· G · Europe

1. The Volga
2. Paris – it is the top of the Eiffel Tower
3. Monaco – it is 3½ miles (5.6 km) long
4. Belgrade
5. Luxembourg
6. Switzerland
7. Brindisi
8. Spain
9. Rotterdam
10. Czechoslovakia
11. The English Channel
12. The Shannon
13. Eros's
14. Hungary
15. Great Britain
16. Yugoslavia
17. Sweden
18. Denmark
19. a) Helsinki
20. Italy
21. In France – near Beauvais. The airship was the R101
22. France
23. Moscow
24. The Atlantic Ocean
25. Romania, which contains Transylvania – he is Count Dracula

2 · E · Mozart & Co

1. William Tell
2. Benjamin Britten (1913–76)
3. Wolfgang Amadeus Mozart (1756–91)
4. Madame Butterfly
5. *A Whiter Shade of Pale*
6. Roger Daltrey, in *Lisztomania* – the composer is Franz Liszt (1811–86)
7. One
8. 'From the New World'
9. *The Magic Flute*
10. *The Dream of Gerontius*
11. The treble clef
12. The words
13. He composed the piano suite *Pictures from an Exhibition* in that year
14. Russian
15. The cello
16. *La Traviata*
17. Herbert von Karajan
18. The 'Unfinished' – the composer is Franz Schubert (1797–1828)
19. George I (1660–1727)
20. Thomas Tallis (c. 1505–85) – *Fantasia on a Theme of Tallis*
21. A minim (a half-note)
22. It is silent
23. Manuel de Falla (1876–1946)
24. Peter Ilich Tchaikovsky (1840–93)
25. Georg Philipp Telemann (1681–1767) – the instrument is the French horn

3 · H · Twentieth Century

1. Hilda – she is Margaret Thatcher
2. Abyssinia (today called Ethiopia) – he is Benito Mussolini (1883–1945)
3. Richard Nixon's
4. Romanov
5. The Treaty of Versailles
6. The Berlin Wall
7. 48 stars
8. The Red Brigade
9. Konrad Adenauer (1876–1967)
10. Shah Mohammad Reza Pahlavi – the Shah of Iran
11. The *Lusitania* – torpedoed on 7 May 1915
12. In Munich
13. Four times
14. Vichy
15. Constantine II
16. Bolivia – he is Che Guevara (1928–67)
17. Albania
18. President Juan Peron died and was succeeded by his wife
19. He became Pope John Paul II
20. That of T. E. Lawrence (Lawrence of Arabia) (1888–1935)
21. In Sarajevo, Yugoslavia – they were Archduke Franz Ferdinand of Austria and his wife
22. The Red Baron – he was Baron Manfred von Richthofen (1882–1918)
23. The SS *Titanic* hit an iceberg and sank
24. In 1983
25. Gabrielle 'Coco' Chanel – the first woman to voluntarily get a suntan

4 · AL · Spies and Sleuths

1. John Le Carré
2. Perry Mason loses
3. Raymond Chandler (1888–1959)
4. James Bond
5. The Saint – Simon Templar
6. Graham Greene
7. A Ronson lighter
8. Ellery Queen
9. James Bond's
10. Bruce Wayne
11. Mickey Spillane
12. The CIA
13. Charlie Chan
14. Sherlock Holmes
15. Belgian
16. Ian Fleming
17. Pinkerton's
18. James Coburn
19. Lord Peter Wimsey
20. Erskine Childers (1870–1922)
21. Wilkie Collins (1824–89)
22. Mycroft
23. George Smiley
24. *The Maltese Falcon*
25. His secretary – Della Street

5 · SN · Birds

1. Scales
2. The albatross
3. The ostrich
4. Two
5. Alfred Hitchcock directed a movie called *The Birds* in 1963
6. The penguin
7. New Zealand – the bird is the kiwi
8. John James Audubon (1785–1851)
9. A swan
10. Richard Burton
11. One swallow
12. The chicken
13. An Arctic tern
14. The kiwi
15. *One Flew Over the Cuckoo's Nest* (1975)
16. Donald Duck
17. *Hotel California*
18. A jackdaw
19. Western Australia
20. The Little Sparrow – she is Edith Piaf (1915–63)
21. A skein
22. Paul Gallico (1897–1976)
23. America
24. Male bee hummingbird
25. Four and twenty

6 · SL · Soccer

1. Yankee Stadium – he is Pele
2. Argentina
3. FIFA – Fédération Internationale de Football Association
4. Bryan Robson scored against France after 27 seconds of play in 1982
5. Norwich City
6. Diego Maradona
7. Italy
8. AC Milan
9. Zico
10. Geoff Hurst in the 1966 final
11. Hungary
12. Jules Rimet
13. 1930
14. Real Madrid
15. Fiji
16. Real Madrid
17. Kenny Dalglish
18. 1984
19. Rio de Janeiro with its Maracana Stadium
20. Europe's leading goal scorer
21. Arsenal
22. Celtic
23. Italy
24. Liverpool
25. France

7 · G · World Tit...

1. S...
2. P...
3. T...
4. A...
5. N... sa...
6. Mexico
7. *New York, New York* – made 1977 and starring Liza Minelli and Robert de Niro
8. Abba
9. In Dallas – they are the stars of the TV soap opera *Dallas*
10. Argentina
11. To Hollywood – they are British band Frankie Goes To Hollywood
12. Audrey Hepburn
13. *Algiers* (1938)
14. Arnhem – Netherlands
15. Singapore
16. *The Canterbury Tales*
17. At Peking – in *55 Days at Peking* (1963)
18. *From Russia With Love* (1963)
19. Harper Valley
20. London – the film is called *An American Werewolf in London*
21. In Marienbad
22. Manhattan
23. St Louis
24. Wisconsin
25. Dooley Wilson – as Sam

8 · E · The Hollywood Greats

1. Breakfast
2. Douglas Fairbanks Jr
3. Natalie Wood (1938–81)
4. Jayne Mansfield (1932–67)
5. Yul Brynner (1915–86)
6. Elizabeth Taylor's breasts
7. Parker
8. Omar Sharif
9. Charlie Chaplin (1889–1977) – the film was made in 1926 but not released because Chaplin threatened legal action
10. Clark Gable (1901–60)
11. 'That was a great game of golf, fellers' – the star was Bing Crosby (1901–77)
12. Michael Caine
13. Jackie Coogan (1914–84) – child star who had his own production company
14. *True Grit*
15. *The Time Machine*
16. *The Graduate*
17. *The Colbys* – she is Barbara Stanwyck
18. Katharine Hepburn – she won the award for *The Lion in Winter* and Streisand for her performance in *Funny Girl*
19. Fred Astaire's
20. Citizen Kane – the actor is Orson Welles
21. By drowning
22. Walt Disney
23. *Gone With The Wind*
24. *A Midsummer Night's Dream* – in which Oberon appears. The actress is Merle Oberon (1911–79)
25. *Straw Dogs*

9 · H · Wild, Wild Women

1 Rose Kennedy (née Fitzgerald)
2 Clementine Churchill
3 b) $1 250 000 – she is Betty Grable (1916–73)
4 Tokyo Rose
5 Mae West
6 'A woman scorned'
7 Samson
8 Bernadette Devlin
9 In Rouen, France – the picture shows Joan of Arc (1412–31), the French patriot and martyr
10 American women
11 Nancy Reagan
12 Spencer
13 The River Thames – she was a Red Indian princess who married an Englishman and died at Gravesend in 1617
14 The parsonage at Haworth, West Yorkshire, England – the sisters are the Brontës
15 Queen Elizabeth I
16 Lot's
17 Dorothy Parker (1893–1967)
18 Pankhurst – Emmeline (1858–1928)founded the Suffragette movement in 1905
19 Archduchess Marie Louise of Austria
20 Mrs Sirimavo Bandaranaike – who first became prime minister of Sri Lanka in 1960
21 Princess Elizabeth (now Queen Elizabeth II)
22 A jolly swagman
23 The Virgin Mary
24 Joseph Stalin (1879–1953)
25 Norma Jean Baker (1926–62)

10 · AL · Bookshelf

1 One thousand and one
2 Eight
3 Chinese
4 Georges Simenon – the detective is Maigret, the actor is Rupert Davies
5 Aramis
6 Jackie Collins – sister of *Dynasty* star Joan
7 Thomas Mann (1875–1955)
8 My Struggle
9 *Nausea*
10 Zorba The Greek
11 Edgar Allen Poe (1809–49)
12 Karamazov – from *The Brothers Karamazov* by Fyodor Dostoevsky
13 Fourteen
14 Franz Kafka (1883–1924)
15 Chilean
16 Alexandre Dumas (1824–95) – the book was *La Dame aux Camellias*, the film was *Camille*, starring Greta Garbo
17 China
18 *One Day in the Life of Ivan Denisovitch*
19 Stephen Leacock (1869–1944)
20 An author
21 The University of Chicago – the book is the *Encyclopaedia Britannica*
22 It attracted the highest price paid for any book or work of art when sold at auction for £8 140 000

11 · SN · Machines

1 Thomas Alva Edison (1847–1931)
2 The windscreen wiper
3 An early clock – made of iron in the fourteenth century
4 Light Amplification by Stimulated Emission of Radiation
5 Raising water
6 Isambard Kingdom Brunel (1806–59)
7 Benjamin Franklin (1706–90)
8 Decypher German codes
9 Sir Christopher Cockerell
10 The cinema – the brothers are Auguste (1862–1954) and Louis (1864–1948) Lumière
11 Boston – Massachusetts
12 The washing machine
13 Vacuum cleaners
14 The AC electric motor – in 1888
15 A radio
16 The jet engine
17 'Mary had a little lamb'
18 The polaroid camera
19 Rover – it had the registration number JET 1
20 Tremors of earthquakes
21 The electrocardiograph
22 It accelerates charged atomic particles
23 The Tardis
24 By means of flowing water
25 Leonardo da Vinci (1452–1519)

12 · SL · Horses and Courses

1 Polo
2 Eight
3 The stirrups
4 Ten
5 The left
6 Ascot
7 Three stallions – *Darley Arabian*, *Byerley Turk* and *Godolphin Barb*
8 Belmont Park – Long Island, New York
9 Longchamp – Paris
10 The Melbourne Cup
11 Newmarket – England
12 William Lee 'Bill' Shoemaker
13 Lester Piggott
14 Virginia Holgate
15 Three-day event, or horse trials
16 Aachen
17 *Shergar*
18 Dr Hackenbush
19 1912
20 Siena
21 Queen Anne (1665–1714)
22 The Grand National
23 The Oaks
24 The Kentucky Derby
25 Dressage

13 · G · Disasters

1 *Queen Elizabeth*
2 Lightning
3 The San Andreas Fault
4 Tenerife in the Canary Islands
5 San Francisco
6 It sank the *Lusitania* in 1915
7 It was lost at sea
8 Los Angeles
9 Steve McQueen
10 Indonesia – the photograph shows the eruption of 1976
11 The *Hindenburg* – which was destroyed in May 1937
12 Amritsar
13 a) 1912
14 Bucharest
15 The Space Shuttle
16 The Richter Scale
17 Tracy
18 India
19 Malfunction of a nuclear power station
20 Jonestown
21 Beirut, Lebanon – it happened when a lorry bomb detonated inside the Marine Barracks
22 The Fastnet Race
23 Salang Tunnel – in Afghanistan
24 Bees
25 Washington – it is Mount St Helens

14 · E · Also known As

1 Mortimer
2 Satchmo – he is Louis Armstrong (1900–71)
3 Twiggy
4 Scott Joplin
5 Archibald Leach – who later became Cary Grant
6 Moby Dick – the whale on whom Herman Melville's novel is based
7 Zorro – strip cartoon and film hero
8 Marie Antoinette (1755–93)
9 Julius – he is better known as Groucho Marx (1890–1977)
10 Sarah Bernhardt (1844–1923) – French actress
11 Billy the Kid (1859–81) legendary American bandit
12 Phineas Taylor Barnum (1810–91) – American showman famous for his flamboyant publicity
13 Lord Haw-Haw – William Joyce (1906–46) was a British traitor who broadcast Nazi propaganda
14 Sammy Davis Jr
15 Frances Gumm – who became famous as Judy Garland (1922–69)
16 Tina Turner
17 Sleeping Beauty
18 Michael Caine
19 Joan Crawford (1906–77)
20 Albert – he was crowned George VI (1895–1952)
21 Johnny Rotten – lead singer with the Sex Pistols
22 John Merrick (1863–90) – known as the Elephant Man
23 Lon Chaney (1906–73)
24 John Wayne (1907–79)
25 Ringo Starr – drummer with The Beatles

15 · H · International Affairs

1 Benito Mussolini (1883–1945)
2 The American Revolution (War of Independence) – it shows the Boston Tea Party (1773)
3 Alaska
4 Andrew Jackson (1808–75) – the picture shows Abraham Lincoln (1809–65)
5 The Politburo
6 The International Red Cross
7 Los Angeles – on 5 June 1968
8 The Japanese surrender in World War
9 Seven
10 London
11 Georgi Malenkov
12 Two – Abraham Lincoln (1865) and William McKinley (1901). The pictur shows Queen Victoria, (1819–1901)
13 Menachem Begin
14 The Cuban Missile Crisis
15 The Office of Strategic Services
16 Moscow
17 St Helena – in the Atlantic
18 The Nationalists
19 Georges Pompidou (1911–74) – it is the museum of contemporary art on the Rue Beaubourg
20 China
21 The United Nations
22 World War I
23 Kampuchea (Cambodia)
24 Raiza
25 Lenin's

16 · AL · Characters

1 Jekyll and Hyde
2 Mrs Hudson
3 The Salvation Army
4 The Invisible Man
5 Leonard Nimoy – who played Spock in *Star Trek*
6 Spanish
7 Two
8 Long John Silver's – in *Treasure Island* by Robert Louis Stevenson (1850–94
9 Galahad
10 Dr Kildare
11 White – he was the eponymous star of Herman Melville's *Moby Dick*
12 Constance – in *Lady Chatterley's Lover* by D. H. Lawrence (1885–1930)
13 F. Scott Fitzgerald (1896–1940)
14 *Women In Love* – by D. H. Lawrence (1885–1930)
15 Dulcinea – in *Don Quixote* by Miguel de Cervantes (1547–1616)
16 Godot – who fails to appear in *Waiting For Godot* by Samuel Beckett
17 Gollum – in *Lord of the Rings* by J. R. Tolkien (1892–1973)
18 A flying school
19 Cinderella
20 Robinson Crusoe
21 Scarlett O'Hara – in *Gone With The Wind* by Margaret Mitchell (1900–4
22 The Godfather
23 Jay – in *The Great Gatsby* by F. Scott Fitzgerald (1896–1940)
24 Adam Bede – the novel is by George Eliot (1819–80)
25 Adam's

17 · SN · Time

1 Six months – with wet and dry seasons of equal length
2 The Mayas
3 Julius Caesar (c. 100–44 BC)
4 Salvador Dali
5 King Alfred
6 The chronometer
7 Caesium
8 They were shorter – about 21 hours long
9 180°
10 Tide
11 One
12 c) 14 September
13 15th century – by Bartholomew Manfredi in 1462
14 May or June – the sign is Gemini, which is generally accepted to cover the period 21 May to 21 June
15 24
16 16
17 Gregory Peck
18 1 minute 40 seconds – or 100 seconds
19 Big Ben – it is officially called the Westminster clock, and is found at the Palace of Westminster, London
20 Ten
21 An astrolabe
22 Seven – New York is five hours behind London, seven hours behind Athens, one hour behind Bermuda and one hour in front of Mexico City
23 A means of dating archeological finds
24 Copenhagen – the clock is the Olsen Clock in the city's Town Hall
25 Salisbury Cathedral's faceless clock dates from 1386, or even earlier

18 SL Time Out

1 The Atlantic – it's one of the beaches of Rio de Janeiro
2 Istanbul – it is the Church of St Sofia
3 Switzerland
4 Belgium
5 Moscow
6 Alberta
7 Brazil
8 Barbados
9 Spain – it is Antonio Gaudi's *Sagrada Familia* in Barcelona
10 Yellowstone National Park – the geyser is Old Faithful
11 Cliff Richard
12 IATA – International Air Transport Association
13 Florida – EPCOT stands for Experimental Community of Tomorrow
14 Provence
15 The Vosges mountains – in eastern France
16 The Maldive Islands
17 Safari
18 The Seychelles
19 Portuguese
20 Mardi Gras – in New Orleans
21 France's Côte d'Azur
22 Neil Simon
23 The Treetops Hotel – 100 miles (160km) north of Nairobi, capital of Kenya
24 San Giminiano
25 France – the island is Mont-St-Michel

19 · G · The Explorers

1 Little America – established at the South Pole in 1933
2 Spain's – the man is Christopher Columbus (1451–1506), the discovery America
3 Plymouth
4 Roald Amundsen and his party
5 St Christopher
6 Swiss
7 Henry Hudson (d. 1611)
8 Christopher Columbus (1451–1506)
9 Amerigo Vespucci (1451–1512) – Florentine explorer after whom America is named
10 Eric Newby – he wrote a book entitled *A Short Walk in the Hindu Kush* about his adventures
11 Vasco da Gama (c. 1460–1524)
12 Sir Ranulph Fiennes – from September 1979 until August 1982 during which time it circumnavigated the globe through both poles
13 Sir Walter Raleigh (1582–1618)
14 St Brendan
15 Kublai Khan (1214–94)
16 Cheng Ho
17 Jacques Cartier (1491–1557)
18 Sir Richard Burton (1829–90)
19 HMS *Beagle*
20 The Sahara – crossing from Sierra Leone to Tangiers
21 The Niger – which he explored between 1795 and 1797
22 Falcon – he is Robert Falcon Scott (1868–1912)
23 The Northwest Passage
24 The second voyage (1772–73)
25 The Dutch

20 · E · Gossip Column

1 Jerry Lee Lewis – who was married to thirteen-year-old Myra Brown
2 Jerry Hall – who left pop star Bryan Ferry for Mick Jagger
3 Sammy Davis Jr
4 Roberto Rossellini – she is Ingrid Bergman (1915–82)
5 1962 – on 5 August
6 Rachmanism – the man is Perec Rachman, who became infamous as a slum landlord
7 Frank Sinatra
8 Because she was discovered to be under age – she is Zsa Zsa Gabor seen with her mother and sisters
9 Eddie Fisher
10 *Jezebel*
11 Robert Wagner
12 Because he was divorced
13 Dr Kurt Waldheim
14 Maria Callas (1923–77)
15 Billie Jean King – American tennis star who admitted the affair
16 Koo Stark – ex-girlfriend of Prince Andrew
17 Liet. E. W. Spencer
18 The Steel Magnolia – she is Rosalynn Carter, wife of Jimmy Carter
19 Fleetwood Mac
20 Princess Grace of Monaco (1929–82) – killed in a car crash
21 Prince Aly Khan – the film star is Rita Hayworth
22 Groucho Marx (1890–1977)
23 Ian Botham
24 Spiro Agnew – American vice-president accused of tax-evasion and accepting bribes
25 Princess Michael of Kent – who discovered her father had been a Nazi

21 · H · Myths and Legends

1 Lady Godiva
2 Camelot
3 The gate of Hades
4 *Mad Max Beyond Thunderdome* – the leader is played by Tina Turner
5 Icarus
6 Noah
7 The Blarney Stone
8 William the Conqueror – he saw Halley's comet in April 1066
9 The left
10 Father Time
11 Remus
12 Astrology
13 Friday – named after Frigg or Freyja
14 Agamemnon
15 Atlas – who was condemned to hold up the sky for his part in the Titans' revolt against the gods
16 *Pygmalion* by George Bernard Shaw
17 Valhalla
18 The prophecies of the oracle – at Delphi
19 The Argonauts
20 T. H. White's *The Once and Future King* – the musical was *Camelot*
21 Sherwood Forest
22 Pegasus
23 Jacques Offenbach (1819–80)
24 Notre Dame – Paris
25 Gene Kelly – Xanadu is a mythical kingdom

22 · AL · Modern Masters

1 Piet Mondrian (1872–1944)
2 Pablo Picasso (1881–1973) – the style is Cubism
3 Sidney Nolan
4 Maurice
5 Gwen John (1876–1939) – sister of Augustus John (1878–1961)
6 Abstract art
7 Andy Warhol
8 *Wham!*
9 Mexican
10 Edgar Degas (1834–1917)
11 Queen Elizabeth II
12 Barbara Hepworth (1903–75)
13 Salvador Dali
14 Paul Gauguin (1853–1903)
15 Belgium
16 Henri Toulouse-Lautrec (1864–1901)
17 Claude Monet (1840–1926) and Edouard Manet (1823–83)
18 Vincent Van Gogh (1853–90)
19 Art Nouveau
20 David Hockney
21 Surrealism
22 Op (or Optical) Art
23 Jackson Pollock (1912–56)
24 Paul Klee (1879–1940)
25 Dadaism

23 · SN · Planet Earth

1 Summer
2 Amber
3 Greenpeace – the ship is the *Rainbow Warrior*
4 Water
5 Natural gas
6 Seven
7 The North Pole
8 The Arctic Circle
9 A stalactite
10 Pioneer 10 – the plaque carries details of the position of the Earth, its inhabitants, and Pioneer's course
11 The ebb tide
12 One ninth
13 South
14 Palaeontology
15 In summer
16 Purple
17 Permafrost
18 Diamonds
19 One per cent
20 AD 1
21 Major Tom – from the song *Space Oddity* by David Bowie
22 The North Pole
23 Marshall McLuhan (1911–82)
24 Dissolved salt
25 He is Gustav Holst (1874–1934) – the English composer of *The Planets*

24 · SL · Athletics

1 Wilma Rudolph
2 Shot put – he is Bruce Bennett, who starred as Tarzan
3 Triple jump
4 Harold Abrahams
5 Javelin
6 Seven events
7 1968
8 Steve Cram
9 On your marks
10 Jesse Owens
11 Ron Clarke
12 Of the 1936 Berlin Olympics
13 Seven
14 Four – he is American athlete Carl Lewis
15 Bob Beamon – whose 29ft 2½in (8.90m) record still stands
16 Zola Budd
17 Greek – he was a shepherd named Spyridon Louis
18 Fifteen miles an hour
19 One lap to go
20 Three feet high
21 He ran it backwards
22 Seventeen years old
23 The foot race
24 Eric Liddell – the film is *Chariots of Fire*
25 Cuban

25 · G · World Records

1 New Guinea
2 Nigeria
3 Lake Ontario
4 The Amazon
5 Hudson Bay
6 China, with 13 frontiers
7 The Sahara
8 Mount Fuji in Japan
9 The USA-Mexico border
10 Reykjavik in Iceland
11 The Northern hemisphere
12 The USSR
13 The Gulf of Mexico
14 The Grand Canyon
15 The Vatican City
16 Canada
17 Second – it's also called K2
18 Damascus, capital of Syria – inhabited for c. 4500 years
19 c) Victoria Nyanza (Lake Victoria)
20 The Pacific Ocean
21 The Portuguese province of Macao – off the southern coast of China
22 The frontier between the USA and Canada
23 Jericho
24 Britain
25 The Caribbean

26 · E · Who Said . . .

1 a) Tallulah Bankhead (1902–68) – the other actresses are b) Lucille Ball and c) Gloria Swanson
2 *To Have and Have Not*
3 Tony Curtis
4 *The Kid*
5 *The Third Man* – although it was never actually spoken in the film
6 Dracula
7 Esther Williams
8 Jimmy Durante (1893–1980)
9 Louis B. Mayer (1885–1957)
10 Olly (Hardy) (1892–1957) said this to Stan (Laurel) (1890–1963)
11 Hedy Lamarr
12 Mr Chips – played in the 1939 movie *Goodbye Mr Chips* by Robert Donat
13 Orson Welles (1915–1986)
14 Fred Astaire and Ginger Rogers
15 'Me no Leica'
16 c) Fred Astaire – the other stars are a) James Cagney and b) Danny Kaye
17 *The Maltese Falcon* – as Sam Spade
18 Julie Andrews
19 Alfred Hitchcock (1899–1980)
20 *A Day at the Races*
21 *Moby Dick*
22 *Some Like It Hot*
23 Mae West
24 Sam Goldwyn (1882–1974)
25 *Rebecca* – the line is addressed to Joan Fontaine

27 · H · Scandal

1 Michelle Triola
2 John Stonehouse – British politician and businessman
3 Marjorie Wallace – crowned Miss World in November 1973
4 He was serving a sentence for possessing marijuana
5 The Bunker Hunt brothers – Nelson and Herbert, who aspired to control the world supply of silver
6 Clifford Irving – the man pictured is Howard Hughes
7 Chamonix
8 Mary Jo Kopechne
9 Christine Keeler
10 Jean-Bedel Bokassa – former president of the Central African Republic
11 Prince Bernhard of the Netherlands
12 Lieutenant Earl Spencer
13 Joyce McKinney
14 Lord Lucan – known as Lucky
15 'Big Bill' Tilden (1893–1953)
16 Alfred Dreyfus (c. 1859–1935)
17 William Randolph Hearst (1863–1951)
18 Christina Crawford – adopted daughter of actress Joan Crawford
19 George IV (1762–1830) – when he was Prince of Wales
20 Sid Vicious – of the Sex Pistols
21 The government of Portugal
22 Watergate – they are Carl Bernstein and Bob Woodward, the two *Washington Post* reporters who uncovered the story
23 Baccarat
24 In the United Kingdom – in 1720
25 The Pope – Pope John Paul I (1912–78)

28 · AL · Quote . . . Unquote

1 Oliver Cromwell (1599–1658)
2 'East is east and west is west'
3 Rudyard Kipling (1865–1936) in *If*
4 Psalm 23
5 Surrender Dorothy
6 *Don Quixote* – by Miguel de Cervantes (1547–1616)
7 *On the Road*
8 James Thurber (1894–1961)
9 Adolf Hitler (1889–1945)
10 Aldous Huxley's *Brave New World* (1932)
11 The last word should be 'wife' not 'diversion'
12 Sherlock Holmes – created by Sir Arthur Conan Doyle and spoken in *The Red-Headed League*
13 *Peter Pan*
14 *A Tale of Two Cities*
15 Lillian Hellman (1907–84)
16 Benjamin Disraeli (1804–81)
17 b) Alfred J. Prufrock
18 A classic
19 Dorothy Parker (1893–1967)
20 James Joyce – the opening words of *Finnegan's Wake*
21 Eleventy-eleventh
22 Hubert Selby Jr's *Last Exit to Brooklyn*
23 'The heart has its reasons' – from Pascal's *Pensées*, used as the title for the memoirs of the Duchess of Windsor (1896–1986)
24 Robert M. Pirsig's *Zen and the Art of Motorcycle Maintenance*
25 Lewis Carroll's *Alice*

29 · SN · The Human Body

1 Ten
2 The liver
3 The uterus – from the Greek word for 'womb' *hustera*
4 The middle finger
5 Four
6 One third
7 The lens
8 Blood – the four groups are A, B, AB and O
9 Smell
10 The eyes
11 206 bones
12 Never
13 Intelligence Quotient
14 The common cold
15 The heel
16 At the tip
17 23
18 Robert Pershing Wadlow (1918–40) the tallest man ever measured, who stood 8ft 11.1ins (2.72m)
19 A finger-print
20 The eardrum
21 Vitamin C
22 40
23 Enamel
24 The real name of the bone is the humerus – thus its nickname
25 Four – the picture shows a gathering quadruplets. Madame Feodor Vassilyev gave birth to 69 children in 27 confinements, producing 16 pairs of twins, 7 sets of triplets and 4 sets of quadruplets

30 · SL · Sporting Greats – The Men

1 Weightlifting
2 O. J. Simpson
3 Franz Beckenbauer
4 Boxing gloves
5 Sir Donald Bradman
6 Floyd Patterson
7 Johann Cruyff – of the Netherlands
8 *The Greatest* – he is Muhammad Ali
9 Gene Tunney
10 Bruce Lee (1940–73)
11 Juan Manuel Fangio
12 Don Larsen
13 Albania
14 Arnold Palmer
15 Gloucestershire
16 Ty Cobb (1886–1961)
17 Aluminium
18 George Hermann (1895–1948)
19 All 49 of them
20 Rod Laver
21 Sir Stanley Matthews
22 Mark Spitz
23 Pele's
24 Jackie Stewart
25 Middleweight – the boxer is Marvin Hagler

31 · G · The Americas

1 French Guiana
2 The Galapagos Islands – the creatures are the giant tortoises which live there
3 George Vancouver (c. 1758–98)
4 Nazca
5 El Salvador
6 One – Ontario
7 USSR
8 Ecuador
9 Brasilia
10 Tin
11 Venezuela
12 Tierra del Fuego
13 The Colorado
14 Maine
15 Peru – the craft is Thor Heyerdahl's *Kon Tiki*
16 1620
17 Mexico City
18 The Mississippi
19 Argentina
20 Honolulu
21 Vermont
22 Chile and Ecuador
23 Lake Michigan
24 Venezuela's Angel Falls – at 3 212ft (979m) they're the highest on earth as well
25 Rockefeller Center

32 · E · The Silver Screen

1 *Romeo and Juliet*
2 Peter Fonda
3 Vanessa Redgrave
4 *Last Tango in Paris*
5 *Psycho*
6 Two
7 Melina Mercouri
8 Charlie Chaplin
9 Theda Bara
10 *Revolution*
11 *Mask*
12 Wolfman Jack
13 Australian – she was Annette Kellerman (1888–1975), the film was *Daughter of the Gods*
14 India
15 *Les Enfants du Paradis*
16 Rainer Werner Fassbinder (1946–85)
17 Julie Andrews
18 Abel Gance's (1889–1982)
19 *The Longest Day*
20 *A Clockwork Orange*
21 *Rosemary's Baby*
22 Gina Lollabrigida
23 Harpo
24 Sergei Eisenstein (1898–1948)
25 *A View To A Kill* – the actor is Patrick MacNee

33 · H · The First Time

1 Alcock and Brown in June 1919
2 Henry Hudson (d. 1611)
3 He was the first black actor to win a Best Actor Oscar – for *Lilies of the Field* in 1963
4 Marilyn Monroe (1926–62)
5 John F. Kennedy (1917–63)
6 Elba
7 Winston Churchill (1874–1965)
8 'Little Boy'
9 Prince Charles
10 The Atlantic – January to July 1969
11 The *Gutenberg Bible*
12 A partridge in a pear tree
13 'Thou shalt have no other gods before me'
14 It was the first feature film to include talking sequences
15 The lightning conductor
16 Queen Elizabeth II
17 Adam Faith
18 Ronald Reagan
19 *Steamboat Willie* (1928)
20 The first link-up in space – it happened on 21 March 1966 when Gemini-8 linked up with the Agena rocket
21 *Midnight Cowboy* (1969)
22 Richard Burton – who married Elizabeth Taylor twice
23 Delaware
24 *The Ten Commandments*
25 *How The West Was Won*

34 · AL · Poet's Corner

1 On the burning deck
2 Emily Dickinson (1830–86)
3 Oscar Wilde (1854–1900)
4 In Westminster Abbey
5 Robert Burns (1759–96)
6 e.e. cummings
7 John Dryden (1631–1700)
8 Alph
9 Gertrude Stein (1874–1946)
10 John Clare (1793–1864)
11 Elizabeth Barrett (1806–61)
12 *Solitude* – by Ella Wheeler Wilcox (1855–1919)
13 Laughing Water
14 Robert Frost (1874–1963)
15 Schiller (1759–1805)
16 W. H. Auden (1907–1973)
17 Skyros – he is Rupert Brooke (1887–1915)
18 John Keats (1795–1821) – he wrote *Ode to a Grecian Urn*
19 'Time's wingèd chariot'
20 Stearns
21 'This Englishwoman'
22 Edward Lear (1812–88)
23 Percy Bysshe Shelley (1792–1822)
24 Samuel Taylor Coleridge (1772–1834)
25 William Blake (1757–1827)

35 · SN · Science for All

1 Nobelium (No) – named after Alfred Nobel (1833–96)
2 Because it's sulphuric acid
3 Salt
4 TNT
5 Sir Isaac Newton (1642–1727)
6 Deoxyribonucleic acid, or DNA
7 Albert Einstein (1899–1955)
8 Acid
9 The first Periodic Table of Elements
10 Du Pont
11 Harder
12 A vacuum
13 The transformation of base metals into gold or silver
14 Mercury
15 Nitrogen
16 Water
17 German silver
18 100 degrees
19 An anaesthetic
20 Red
21 Jean Michel Jarre – his composition was *Oxygene*
22 Diamond – which is mainly carbon
23 *Back to the Future* – Steven Speilberg's film starring Michael J. Fox and Christopher Lloyd
24 Fire
25 Bronze

36 · SL · Tennis

1 Kevin Curren
2 The Swedish royal family
3 a) 55 – he is Bobby Riggs
4 The Federation Cup
5 Le Jeu de Paume – the French name for real or royal tennis, from which tennis evolved. The painting *The Oath of the Tennis Court* is by David
6 Margaret Smith-Court – in the Australian Championships
7 Richard Sears – who won the first seven from 1881 to 1887
8 Andrea Jaeger – when she won the 1981 mixed doubles aged 15 years and 339 days
9 Richard
10 78ft (23.77m)
11 Marianne Simionescu
12 Tim and Tom Gullikson
13 World Championship Tennis
14 He became the first man to achieve the Grand Slam
15 Maureen 'Little Mo' Connolly (USA)
16 *Monsieur Hulot's Holiday* (1952)
17 After the 1924 games
18 In 1973
19 Tracy Austin – aged 16 years and 271 days
20 c) 4 – Czechoslovakian, Bohemia-Moravian, Egyptian and British, as a result of political events and his status as a refugee
21 Yannick Noah
22 John and Tracy Austin
23 The United States Tennis Association
24 Czechoslovakia
25 In 1982

37 · G · The Orient

1 Tibet
2 India
3 The Burma Road
4 Honshu
5 Afghanistan and Pakistan
6 Calcutta
7 *A Passage To India* – the actor is Victor Banerjee
8 China and Japan
9 Shanghai
10 Saigon
11 Indonesia
12 January
13 Samarkand
14 The Caspian Sea
15 Siam (today's Thailand)
16 The Yangtze
17 Israel
18 In Hong Kong harbour – it is the Dragon Boat Race
19 a) The Moluccas – a group of islands in Indonesia, famous for nuts and cloves
20 Hinduism
21 Sikhism
22 The Pakistani rupee
23 The Occident
24 a) north
25 Angkor Wat

38 · E · Making Music

1 By wind passing across the strings
2 The violin
3 Slowly
4 The Moog Synthesizer
5 Jimi Hendrix (1942–70)
6 Stu Sutcliffe
7 Ravi Shankar
8 Jethro Tull
9 Jimi Hendrix (1942–70)
10 Green
11 A violin – the clown is Grock, who was played by Adrien Wettach (1880–1959)
12 Cremona
13 Adolphe Sax (1814–94)
14 The tuba
15 A balalaika
16 An organ scholarship – he is Dudley Moore
17 Ignace Jan Paderewski (1860–1941)
18 David Bowie
19 New York City, with the Metropolitan Opera House, at the Lincoln Center
20 'Happy Birthday'
21 The ukelele – he is George Formby (1905–61)
22 Paul McCartney
23 Japan
24 The oboe
25 Johanna ('Jenny') Maria Lind (1820–87)

39 · H · Law and Order

1 Carmel – the man is Clint Eastwood
2 France
3 Pope John Paul II
4 Judge Roy Bean
5 Pat Garrett
6 Wyatt Earp
7 Sir Robert Peel (1788–1850) – who established the Metropolitan Police Force in 1829
8 King John (1167–1216)
9 Gerald Ford
10 Inspector Clouseau – played by Peter Sellers (1925–80)
11 Andrew Jackson (1767–1845)
12 Left-handed
13 The body
14 *Oliver Twist* – the character is Mr Bumble
15 Australia
16 Leaving the scene of an accident
17 Franklin D. Roosevelt (1884–1945)
18 Harrison Ford
19 a) Telly Savalas – who reached number one in the British charts in March 1975
20 Garry Gilmore's
21 The second
22 The UK – the territory is Gibraltar
23 Murphy's Law
24 From Ur – dating from c. 2110 BC
25 A computer made by IBM

40 · AL · Words, Words, Words

1 Gamma
2 Negro
3 English
4 Where are you going
5 Scampo
6 German
7 N
8 A
9 The Rosetta Stone – which provided the key to Egyptian hieroglyphics
10 Aloha
11 From right to left
12 Paprika
13 Amen
14 Newspeak
15 Lightning war
16 German
17 24
18 The siesta
19 The Cambodian alphabet has 72 letters
20 Cha
21 The hoping, or hopeful, one
22 A love letter
23 The Prince of Wales's
24 On the Isle of Man
25 They are kamikaze pilots and kamikaze means 'divine wind'

41 · SN · Numbers and Statistics

1 1000
2 Latitudes 40°–50° South which are characterized by strong winds
3 49
4 a) 12
5 Zero
6 The cubit
7 A contour line
8 The Charge of the Light Brigade – at Balaklava in 1854
9 Two
10 The same bust measurement – they are Jayne Mansfield (1932–67) and Marie Antoinette (1755–93)
11 b) 985ft (300.53m)
12 Ten
13 Binary digit
14 Robert Powell
15 That is the temperature at which book paper spontaneously ignites – the plot centres on the destruction of literature in a future society
16 144
17 100 times
18 One foot
19 12
20 c) 1635
21 30 years of marriage
22 Absolute zero
23 MM
24 20
25 24 – the man is Gene Pitney

42 · SL · Champions

1 Bob Champion – played by John Hurt in the film
2 A footrace
3 Cassius X – and later to Muhammad Ali
4 John McEnroe
5 Joe Davis (1903–78)
6 Willie Shoemaker
7 The Hockenheim circuit, West Germany – the driver was Jim Clark (1937–68)
8 41
9 c) 750cc
10 Joe Louis
11 The cheetahs
12 Badminton
13 New Zealander
14 Muhammad Ali
15 The French team – they have won it on 12 occasions
16 Mother's Day
17 Yellow
18 His moustache
19 Guillermo Vilas of Argentina
20 Eusebio
21 Downhill skiing
22 Anatoly Karpov
23 Pakistan
24 Sumo wrestling
25 Rodeo

43 · G · Site Seeing

1 The Leaning Tower of Pisa
2 Nairobi
3 Indonesia
4 Prague
5 Rio de Janeiro
6 Athens's
7 The Palace of Versailles
8 Minnesota
9 London's British Museum
10 The running of the bulls
11 St Peter's – Vatican City
12 July 4 1776
13 Intourist
14 Agra
15 Turkey
16 The Hanging Gardens of Babylon
17 The Rialto
18 Brussels
19 British
20 Queen Victoria's husband, Prince Albert (1819–61) – it is the Royal Albert Hall in London
21 Jerusalem
22 Wiltshire – it is Stonehenge, a prehistoric monument
23 The Great Pyramid of Khufu
24 The famous terracotta army of soldiers
25 Tokyo – none of the other Disneyland sites are in capital cities

44 · E · Dance

1 It was written for baby elephants – to be performed in the circus ring
2 Margot Fonteyn
3 *Swan Lake*
4 Shirley MacLaine and Anne Bancroft
5 Dame Ninette de Valois
6 Leslie Caron
7 St Marylebone – London
8 Danish
9 Odile
10 Michael Clarke
11 Carole Lombard (1908–42)
12 The last Waltz – it was used as a dance hall during the war
13 *Fantasia* – the picture shows the feet of the dancing ostriches
14 Vaslav – he is Nijinsky (1888–1950)
15 Juliet Prowse
16 None – it's a solo
17 They write down dances – using special notation systems to keep a record of the steps and moves of a ballet
18 Mata Hari – the stage name of Margarete Zelle (1876–1917), who spied for the Germans during World War I
19 Four
20 Leningrad
21 No one – it has no music
22 Lola Montez (1818–61) – Irish dancer and adventuress
23 Fred Astaire – she is better known as Ginger Rogers
24 Anna Pavlova (1885–1931)
25 $10 million – she is Cyd Charisse

45 · H · When Was It?

1 May – for Sport Aid
2 b) 1860
3 1933
4 1066
5 August – on 6 August 1945, to be precise
6 b) 1969
7 1900 – she is HRH Queen Elizabeth, the Queen Mother
8 c) 1917
9 The Battle of the Boyne was fought
10 1941 – the writer is Virginia Woolf (1882–1941)
11 c) 1960 – the sailor is Sir Francis Chichester (1901–72)
12 Charles Lindbergh (1902–74) – he made the first solo non-stop transatlantic flight
13 The Hudson Bay Company
14 The Montgolfier brothers made their first flight in a hot air balloon
15 1981
16 c) 1979
17 1901
18 a) 1914
19 a) 1963
20 The Domesday Book
21 St Crispin's Day – 25 October
22 Mrs Indira Gandhi was assassinated
23 1924
24 June – from the fifth to the tenth
25 b) 1976

46 · AL · Old Masters

1 J. M. W. Turner (1775–1851)
2 Fresco – painted on walls or ceilings before the plaster is dry
3 Raphael – the day was 6 April
4 64 – he is Rembrandt (1606–69)
5 Four and a half years
6 Crete
7 Sir Joshua Reynolds (1723–92)
8 Peter
9 Giotto (1267–1337)
10 13
11 Botticelli (1445–1510) – the painting is the *Birth of Venus*
12 Belgium
13 Eyebrows
14 Canaletto (1697–1768)
15 Rembrandt (1606–69)
16 St Peter's – Rome
17 Velasquez (1599–1660)
18 Jacques Louis David (1748–1825)
19 John Constable (1776–1837) – it is entitled *The Leaping Horse*
20 Pieter – they were called The Elder (1525–69) and Hell Brueghel (1564–1638)
21 Jan Vermeer (1632–75)
22 Giorgio Vasari (1511–74)
23 Caravaggio (1569–1609)
24 Henry VIII
25 George Stubbs (1724–1806) – the picture shows one of his drawings for *The Anatomy of a Horse*

47 · SN · Land Animals

1 Beat their chests
2 The rattlesnake
3 The tiger
4 Robert the Bruce (1274–1329) – the creature that inspired him was a spider
5 The elephant
6 A beaver
7 Jaguars
8 None of them
9 Testicles
10 The opossum
11 The giant tortoise
12 The camel family – the creature is a llama
13 Four
14 The duckbilled platypus
15 A wolf
16 Rudyard Kipling (1865–1936)
17 'Earth-pig'
18 Slatey grey
19 The antelope family
20 The caribou or reindeer
21 The ears
22 The Abominable Snowman
23 The giraffe
24 Mrs Tiggywinkle
25 The Romans – the creature is an edible dormouse

48 · SL · Gaming and Gambling

1 Chemin de fer
2 The jack of diamonds
3 15
4 Five aces
5 121
6 Nathan Detroit – in the musical *Guys and Dolls*, adapted from Damon Runyan's story by Joseph Mankiewicz and Frank Loesser
7 Poker – he is American president Harry Truman (1884–1972)
8 Atlantic City – New Jersey, with the Resorts International Casino
9 Blackjack or Twenty-One
10 A deck of cards
11 Three of a kind
12 Seven
13 The 'Kalamazoo'
14 Wild Bill Hickock
15 Bingo
16 Thirty-five to one
17 Robert Shaw
18 Five cents
19 A shooter
20 $5000
21 Slot machines
22 Nine, ten and eleven
23 75
24 Baccarat
25 Five

49 · G · Africa

1 Lake Victoria or Victoria Nyanza
2 Zaire
3 The Atlantic
4 Khartoum – capital of Sudan
5 Zanzibar
6 Morocco
7 Alexandria – he wrote *Alexandria Quartet* from 1957–60
8 Sierra Leone ('Lion Mountain ridge')
9 David Livingstone (1813–73)
10 Morocco
11 France
12 C. S. Forester's (1899–1966)
13 Alan Paton
14 Webster's Dictionary
15 The Sudan
16 Third – after Asia and America
17 Madagascar
18 In Libya – at Al Aziziyah on 13 September 1922. It was 136.4°F (58°C)
19 Libya – it was said that he had received money from Libyan sources
20 Ghana
21 Edgar Rice Burroughs (1875–1950)
22 Hippopotamus comes from the Greek meaning 'river horse'
23 Clarence
24 Henry Morton Stanley (1841–1904)
25 Camelopard

50 · E · Blockbusters

1 Francis Ford Coppola
2 *The Seven Year Itch* – the actress is Marilyn Monroe (1926–62)
3 *The Sound of Music*
4 George Lucas
5 Sylvester Stallone
6 Barbra Streisand the film was *Yentl*
7 Seven – the actor is Roger Moore
8 *The Exorcist*
9 Three – Tamara de Treaux, Pat Bilson and Matthew de Merritt. The character is E.T., from the film of the same name
10 Chewbacca
11 *Zulu*
12 El Cid
13 Gremlins – from the film of the same name
14 *Around The World In 80 Days*
15 *Gandhi* – an estimated 300 000 people turned out for the funeral scene
16 *Giant*
17 *Chances Are*
18 *Lawrence of Arabia* – the picture shows Vivien Leigh and Clark Gable in *Gone With The Wind*
19 *The Man Who Would Be King*
20 Mario Puzo
21 John Williams
22 A brahman bull
23 *Tales of the South Pacific*
24 *Tomorrow Belongs To Me*
25 Clyde

51 · H · Wars and Weapons

1 The Spanish Civil War
2 Egypt's
3 The French Foreign Legion
4 The American Civil War
5 General Douglas MacArthur (1880–1964)
6 The *Enterprise*
7 World War II
8 Hannibal
9 The War of the Roses
10 Camels
11 World War II
12 The Crusades
13 The Vietnam War
14 France and Spain
15 Belgium – the cartoon is of the Duke of Wellington
16 a) 1916 – on 15 September on the River Somme
17 World War I
18 Samuel Colt (1814–62)
19 R2 D2
20 An ancient missile engine for hurling stones etc.
21 11 – the armistice was signed at the 11th hour of the 11th day of the 11th month, of 1918
22 The Hundred Years War between England and France 1337–1453
23 Audie Murphy (1924–71)
24 The Crimean War – the picture is of Florence Nightingale (1820–1910)
25 The Mason-Dixon Line

52 · AL · The Ancients

1 The Gorgons
2 The fox
3 Troy – it is the wooden horse, in which Greek soldiers were hidden. They destroyed the city
4 Twelve
5 Narcissus
6 His right heel
7 Ambrosia
8 Pandora's
9 Virgil (70 BC–19 BC)
10 The Roman civilization
11 Taoism
12 Alexander Pope (1688–1744)
13 Rome – it is Trajan's Column
14 Electra, daughter of Agamemnon
15 Ovid (43 BC–AD 18)
16 By ensuring that her prophecies were not believed
17 Aeschylus (525 BC–456 BC)
18 Poseidon
19 Crete – they are bull-jumping
20 Mycenae
21 b) Doric
22 *Ben Hur*
23 Robert Graves (1895–1986)
24 The death of Alexander the Great
25 Spartacus

53 · SN · Plant Life

1 The cedars of Lebanon
2 The air
3 Water
4 In its leaves
5 The dandelion
6 The opium poppy
7 Kew Gardens in London
8 The orchid
9 From the bark
10 Pulverized tobacco
11 Sequoiah
12 The picture shows a white cabbage, and *Pieris brassicae* is the cabbage white butterfly
13 The mushroom
14 Seeds
15 Genetics
16 Triffids – from *The Day of the Triffids*
17 Yew trees
18 In the USSR
19 Niger – it is 31 miles (50 km) from any other tree
20 George Orwell (Eric Blair) (1903–50)
21 The crocus
22 The rose – she is Bette Midler who starred in the film *The Rose*
23 b) south
24 China
25 The Swedish scientist Carl Linnaeus (1707–78)

54 · SL · Motor Sports

1 Le Mans
2 Volkswagen's – Formula Vee was the first class for cars built round standard one-make components
3 The Isle of Man
4 The Netherlands
5 Memorial Day – 30 May
6 The Bonneville Salt Flats
7 Mario Andretti
8 Formula One
9 Le Mans Start
10 *The Great Race*
11 France – in 1906
12 Belgrade
13 In a Honda
14 Long Beach – California
15 The Pike's Peak hillclimb – first held in 1916
16 The Mini Cooper S
17 Ettore Bugatti (1882–1967)
18 Ferrari – which has been competing since 1948
19 Tyrrell – the car was the Tyrell Project 34/2, first run in 1976
20 Jackie Stewart in 1979
21 Lotus
22 Jack Brabham – who won the title driving his Repco-Brabham in 1966
23 Belgian
24 Graham Hill (1929–75)
25 Moto-Cross (also known as scrambling)

55 · G · Highspots

1 James Hilton
2 They are the first to have stood on the peak of the world's highest mountain, Mount Everest – they are Tenzing Norgay and Edmund Hillary
3 Aconcagua – Argentina. The highest peak in the Andes at 22 834ft (6 960m)
4 Mount McKinley – the highest mountain in North America at 20 320ft (6 194m)
5 Tanzania – Kilimanjaro is 19 340ft (5 894m) high
6 Mount Ararat – in Turkey. The vessel is Noah's Ark
7 Mount Olympus
8 Bolivia – the city is La Paz (its *de facto* capital)
9 Mount Sinai
10 Island of Martinique
11 Rio de Janeiro in Brazil
12 Sir George Everest (1790–1866) – sometime Surveyor General of India
13 Austria and Italy
14 Italy
15 The Urals
16 In Canada – the CN Tower in Toronto
17 In Afghanistan – through the Hindu Kush
18 George Washington, after whom Mount Washington in the White Mountains is named
19 Mount Vesuvius
20 Theodore Roosevelt (1858–1919)
21 *The Eiger Sanction*
22 The Sears Tower – in Chicago, Illinois in 1974. The picture shows the Empire State Building in New York
23 John Denver
24 Trafalgar Square – the picture shows Nelson's Column, London
25 Lake Titicaca in South America – 12 506ft (3 811m) above sea level

56 · E · The Wild West

1 Calamity Jane
2 Ty Hardin
3 Tombstone – Arizona
4 Roy Rogers
5 *High Noon* (1952)
6 Louis L'Amour
7 Sean Connery – the movie was *Shalako* (1968), the leading lady Brigitte Bardot
8 Tonto – the Lone Ranger's companion
9 Steve McQueen (1930–80)
10 The Pony Express
11 Chingachgook
12 Marlene Dietrich
13 *Rawhide*
14 John Ford
15 Davy Crockett
16 Calgary
17 Doc
18 Lee Marvin
19 Frank James
20 James Drury
21 William Cody (1846–1917)
22 Robert Redford
23 Burt Bacharach – the song was *Raindrops Keep Falling on My Head* in *Butch Cassidy and the Sundance Kid*
24 Rin Tin Tin
25 *Blazing Saddles*

57 · H · Battles and Rebellions

1 The army of the USSR
2 The Crimean War
3 The Battle of Little Big Horn (1876)
4 Lord Cornwallis (1732–1805) – he surrendered to George Washington (1732–99)
5 *I Wish I Was in Dixieland*
6 Field Marshal Montgomery (1887–1976) and Field Marshal Rommel (1891–1944)
7 Tchaikovsky's *1812 Overture*
8 Fletcher Christian
9 Waterloo
10 China
11 The Sudan – British troops defeated the forces of the Mahdi at the Battle of Atbara in 1898
12 Belgium
13 Kenya
14 Battle of Bosworth Field (1485)
15 Joan of Arc
16 The Winter Palace, Leningrad – during the Bolshevik Revolution (1917)
17 Africa – they landed at Algiers and Casablanca
18 Sunday 7 December 1941
19 Constantinople (today Istanbul) – former capital of the Byzantine empire
20 Battle of Lepanto (1571)
21 General John J. Pershing (1860–1948)
22 Battle of Hastings (1066)
23 The Russian Revolution of 1917 – the man is Lenin (1870–1924)
24 The Battle of the Bulge (1944–5)
25 The Emperor Claudius (10 BC–AD 54)

58 · AL · Men in Print

1 Hans Christian Andersen (1807–75)
2 A French poodle
3 *Tropic of Cancer* and *Tropic of Capricorn*
4 *Animal Farm*
5 Ken Kesey
6 *Steppenwolf*
7 *Oliver's Story*
8 Sir Arthur Conan Doyle (1859–1930) – named his character Sherlock Holmes
9 Vincent van Gogh (1853–90)
10 Alexander Solzhenitsyn
11 *Uncle Remus*
12 *The Guinness Book of Records*
13 *The Two Towers*
14 *The Mystery of Edwin Drood*
15 Tuberculosis
16 Alvin Toffler
17 *Papillon*
18 Edgar Allen Poe's (1809–49)
19 Nevil Shute
20 Jude – from *Jude the Obscure*
21 *Shogun*
22 *The Poseidon* – in *The Poseidon Adventure*
23 *Armageddon*
24 Joseph Conrad (1857–1924)
25 Norman Mailer – the star is Marilyn Monroe (1926–62)

59 · SN · Medicine

1 The mosquito
2 Valium
3 A carcinogen
4 Near-sighted
5 Rabies
6 A cold
7 The moment of conception – demonstrated by a sea-urchin
8 Yeast
9 Welby – in the TV series *Marcus MD*
10 Aspirin
11 Three times a day
12 Polio
13 Morphine
14 He was hanged because of it – he is Dr Crippen (1862–1910), who murdered his wife and escaped to America on board an Atlantic liner, only to be caught because of the newly-installed wireless
15 Hippocrates
16 Hypoxemia, or lack of blood to the brain
17 Richard Chamberlain
18 German measles
19 Leukaemia – the film is *Love Story*
20 The male
21 Influenza
22 Dr Christiaan Barnard
23 Electrocardiogram
24 Motor Neurone Disease – he is actor David Niven (1909–84)
25 Bubonic Plague

60 · SL · Golf

1 Mary Queen of Scots (1542–87)
2 Four and a quarter inches (106 mm)
3 Greg Norman
4 Wood
5 Gary Player
6 Bernhard Langer
7 Three strokes fewer than par for a ho
8 In Japan – the seventh hole on the Sano course, Satsuki GC is 909 yd (831 m) long
9 A three wood
10 The Augusta National Golf Course, Georgia
11 Four
12 1983 – the man is Bob Hope, whose British Classic Golf Tournament was last played in 1983 after accusations o financial mismanagement
13 Nine
14 The match between the universities o Oxford and Cambridge
15 Palm Springs
16 On a mound or pinch of sand
17 Lee Trevino
18 Tom Watson
19 Four inches (102 mm)
20 1979
21 Five
22 Peru – the course is over 14 000 ft (4267 m) above sea level
23 The PGA – the Professional Golfers' Association championship
24 A putt
25 The British Open

61 · G · The Seven Seas

1 Pepi – the film was based on the life o sea captain Geoffrey Thorpe
2 The Marianas Trench – 6.78 miles (10.91kms) deep
3 *Double-Eagle V*
4 The Mediterranean Sea
5 Sir Francis Drake (c. 1540–96) – who renamed the ship the *Golden Hind* during his 1577–80 voyage
6 The Arctic Ocean
7 Vitus Bering (1681–1741) – Danish navigator
8 *The Cruel Sea* – by Nicholas Monsarra
9 The Black Sea
10 Iran
11 a) 80%
12 Bluto
13 Portugal – Henry the Navigator (1394–1460) built an observatory and school of navigation
14 The Atlantic
15 The Caspian Sea – 143 550 miles² (371 800km²)
16 *Sailing* – the singer is Rod Stewart
17 b) 60°S
18 Venice
19 Isambard Kingdom Brunel (1806–59)
20 The Indian Ocean
21 Poseidon
22 The Strait of Gibraltar
23 Sea of Marmara
24 Canada
25 Two hours each – the other watches are each of four hours

62 · E · Rock'n'Roll

1 Iowa – he is Buddy Holly (1936–59)
2 Led Zeppelin
3 Bill Haley and his Comets
4 Aaron
5 Brian Jones
6 Duane Eddy – one of the first rock stars to use an electric guitar
7 The E Street Band – Bruce Springsteen is pictured
8 Queen
9 Phil and Don – Everly, who together formed the Everly Brothers
10 The Crickets
11 Cliff Richard
12 Black – from their hit single *Paint It Black*
13 The Candystore Prophets played the music for the Monkees early hits – the Monkees were a group of actors who did not at first perform their own songs
14 Lefthanded – he is Jimi Hendrix (1942–70)
15 Alice Cooper
16 Eric Clapton
17 Status Quo
18 *Blue Hawaii*
19 Roger Daltrey
20 Herman Hesse (1877–1962) – German poet and novelist
21 *Piper At The Gates of Dawn* – by Pink Floyd. The book was written by Kenneth Grahame (1859–1922)
22 Jerry Lee Lewis
23 Billy Fury
24 Adam and the Ants
25 Teddy – together they formed the Beverley Sisters

63 · H · Heads of State

1 Nicholas Breakspear (Adrian IV) (c.1115–59)
2 Lenin (1870–1924)
3 Austria
4 Gamel Abdel Nasser (1918–70) – President of Egypt
5 Louis XIV (1638–1715)
6 He was killed in a car crash
7 He was his son-in-law
8 Haile Selassie – Emperor of Ethiopia (1930–74)
9 Caesar
10 Hawaii
11 Japan
12 Ludwig II of Bavaria (1845–86)
13 Ethelred II (968–1016) – he was known as 'Unready' because he was never able to foresee events and prepare for them
14 The Black Prince (1330–76)
15 Sir Wilfred Laurier (1841–1919)
16 Jawaharlal Nehru (1889–1964)
17 Grand Master la Vallette – he defended the island against a Turkish seige in 1565 and gave his name to Valetta
18 Augustine, first Archbishop of Canterbury (d.604), later canonized
19 a) third – he is Thomas Jefferson (1743–1826)
20 Lady Jane Grey (1537–54) – Queen of England for nine days in 1553
21 Pop star Elton John's – the future head of state is HRH Prince Charles
22 Queen Anne (1665–1714)
23 French – he was Gregory XI (1329–78)
24 France
25 Sailing   the king was Constantine II

64 · AL · Modern Fiction

1 Mordor
2 Italy
3 Evelyn Waugh (1903–66)
4 Catch-22
5 *1984*
6 *Jonathan Livingstone Seagull*
7 Her novel *The Prime of Miss Jean Brodie*
8 *The Godfather* – the actor is Marlon Brando, photographed in 1947
9 *The Devil's Alternative*
10 Harvard
11 *Of Human Bondage*
12 Irwin Shaw's
13 E. M. Forster (1879–1970)
14 Alice Springs – Australia
15 *Gentlemen Prefer Blondes* – by Anita Loos
16 Slavery
17 *Midnight Cowboy* – Dustin Hoffman played Rico Rizzo
18 L. P. Hartley (1895–1972) – the novel is *The Go-Between*
19 Baron Von Richthofen – the novelist is D. H. Lawrence (1885–1930) who was married to Von Richthofen's cousin
20 Denis Wheatley
21 *The Mirror Crack'd From Side To Side* – from *The Lady of Shalott*. The novel is called *The Mirror Crack'd*
22 Amis – the father is Kingsley, the son Martin
23 Adrian Mole – who is the creation of Sue Townsend
24 *The French Lieutenant's Woman*
25 Jeffrey Archer – author of such books as *Cain and Abel* and also Deputy Chairman of the Conservative Party

65 · SN · Space

1 Stanley Kubrick
2 Edwin 'Buzz' Aldrin Jr
3 Project Mercury
4 Star Wars – SDI stands for Strategic Defence Initiative
5 7 – the programme is *Blake's Seven*
6 Venus
7 Alan B. Shepard – who played the first game of golf on the moon in 1961
8 A black hole
9 Two
10 France
11 Czech – he was Vladimir Remek who flew in Soyuz 28 in March 1978
12 Britain
13 Apollo 8 – made the first orbit of the moon in 1968
14 Eagle
15 Three
16 Valentina Tereshkova – who flew in Vostok 6 in June 1963
17 Apollo 1
18 Vulcan – he is Mr Spock, half-human and half-Vulcan, from *Star Trek*
19 H. G. Wells (1866–1946)
20 Werner von Braun (1912–77)
21 Edward H. White II in Gemini 4, in June 1965
22 None
23 Australia
24 Mars
25 Leika – she was launched into space in 1957 aboard Sputnik II

66 · SL · Cheers!

1 Amoroso
2 Champagne and stout – Guinness for preference
3 White
4 A margarita
5 The Bloody Mary
6 Dry
7 Gin
8 Coffee beans
9 Green
10 Celery
11 A triangle
12 Tawny
13 Table wine
14 Salt, tequila, lemon
15 Champagne
16 Benedictine and brandy
17 Grand Marnier
18 Right
19 Aquavit
20 The martini
21 Indian clubs – used for exercise
22 Portugal
23 Hungary
24 Champagne – he is Dom Perignon, inventor of the method Champagnoise
25 Shaken but not stirred

67 · G · World Symbols

1 KLM – the national airline of the Netherlands
2 Blue
3 Tokyo – Narita Airport
4 Eleven
5 The edelweiss
6 The scarlet pimpernel
7 Nepal
8 Kentucky
9 The skull and crossbones
10 Christianity
11 The crescent shape of the new moon
12 The Plimsoll Mark
13 Green
14 Canada – it is the beaver
15 CD
16 Gold
17 The greyhound
18 The leek
19 National Aeronautics and Space Agency
20 Denmark's
21 The cock
22 Athene – goddess of wisdom
23 Cyprus
24 The Sunshine State
25 Yin and Yang

68 · E · Cartoon Time

1 Tom and Jerry
2 Penguins
3 *The Lady and the Tramp*
4 Jellystone National Park
5 Deputy Dawg
6 A basinful of champagne
7 Bugs Bunny
8 *Fantasia*
9 Swee'pea
10 *The Jungle Book*
11 *Bambi*
12 *Gulliver's Travels*
13 *The Fox and the Hound* – which cost $10 million
14 Goofy
15 Donald Duck's
16 Baloo the Bear
17 *One Hundred and One Dalmations* – she is Cruella de Vil
18 Speedy Gonzales
19 United Productions of America, creators of Mr Magoo, Gerald McBoing and Pete Hothead
20 *Snow White and the Seven Dwarfs*
21 *Top Cat*
22 Sylvester
23 Walt Disney used his own voice
24 Woody Woodpecker
25 Pinocchio – his nose grows longer

69 · H · Ancient Worlds

1 Alexander the Great (356–323 BC)
2 The Persians
3 The Emperor Claudius (10 BC–AD 54)
4 Hannibal (247–182 BC) – Carthaginian soldier
5 The lighthouse on the island of Pharos, built in 270 BC but destroyed by earthquakes
6 Greek – she is Cleopatra (69–30 BC)
7 The construction of the Great Wall of China – completed c.200 BC
8 Three
9 Vesuvius
10 Horse racing
11 c) 45 000 – it is the Coliseum in Rome, built cAD 75–80
12 Plato (c.427–c.347 BC)
13 Pontius Pilate
14 Babel
15 Gnaeus Pompey (106–48 BC)
16 Socrates (before 469–399 BC)
17 Aqueducts
18 Constantine (c.274–337)
19 After – between AD 800 and 900
20 Knossos – on Crete
21 January – named after Janus who presides over the 'entrance' to the year
22 Londinium
23 Britain – he was elected consul in AD 77 and followed as governor of Britain
24 Tigris and Euphrates – Mesopotamia is the Greek for 'between the rivers'
25 Athens – it is the Parthenon, built in 447–32 BC on the Acropolis

70 · AL · Settings

1 The Louvre
2 In his bathroom – it is the *Mona Lisa* by Leonardo da Vinci (1452–1519)
3 In Florence – Italy
4 Never Never Land
5 Twelve Oaks
6 Jay Gatsby
7 Two
8 *Sleuth*
9 Spain
10 The Floss – in *The Mill on the Floss* by George Eliot (1819–80)
11 Bonn
12 Australia
13 Lancashire – the artist is L. S. Lowry (1887–1976)
14 Montmartre
15 Earth
16 Mars
17 Michelangelo (1475–1564)
18 *Twelfth Night*
19 *Goodbye Columbus*
20 In Paris and London
21 The world's largest painting
22 In Malibu – California
23 Florence – from the film of E. M. Forster's novel *A Room with a View*
24 Flatford Mill – painted by John Constable (1776–1837)
25 Upon Westminster Bridge

71 · SN · Flight

1 London
2 Amelia Earhart (1898–1937)
3 The speed of sound
4 Paris
5 Two
6 W.E. Johns – the air ace is Captain James Bigglesworth, known as Biggles
7 Vertical Take-Off and Landing
8 Orville Wright – whose passenger was killed in a crash in 1908
9 The Soviet Union's Aeroflot
10 Le Bourget, Paris
11 *The Dam Busters*
12 Monaco – the competitions were held for seaplanes
13 The first Flying Doctor Service
14 The autogyro
15 The first London to Paris air race
16 *Flying Down To Rio* (1933)
17 Louis Blériot (1872–1936) – the plane was called *La Berline de Deutsch*
18 The Soviet Union's – the plane was the Tupolev TU-144
19 Howard Hughes himself
20 The Tornado
21 The German airline, then called Deutsche Luft-Hansa, in May 1926
22 Rio de Janeiro, via Dakar in Senegal
23 None
24 *Enola Gay*
25 The French Revolution – the balloonists are the Montgolfier brothers

72 · SL · World Games

1 Roller derby
2 Tungsten
3 Lawn bowls
4 Six
5 Fencing
6 Skydiving
7 Four
8 Skateboarding
9 Surfers
10 Chess
11 Karate
12 The heart
13 The clay pigeon
14 King Dyal – who supports the West Indies
15 Bullfighting
16 Soccer teams
17 Weightlifting
18 A horse race in the rain
19 The Russian invasion of Afghanistan
20 Judo
21 Cyclocross
22 World Boxing Council
23 Archery
24 The Tour de France
25 Blue

73 · G · Islands

1 Goat Island
2 Melos
3 On the island of St Helena – (where Napoleon Bonaparte died) 1 320 miles (2 120kms) away
4 Mauritius – the bird is the dodo
5 In the pancreas – they are groups of small granular cells that secrete insulin
6 Sicily – it is Mount Etna. The illustration shows its eruption in 1669
7 The islands of Western Samoa – where Robert Louis Stevenson (1850–94) died on the island of Upolu
8 The tropic of Cancer
9 99 years
10 Hispaniola
11 Berne – in Switzerland
12 Great Britain
13 The Falkland Islands
14 The flag of the United Kingdom
15 The Hebrides Overture – the view is of Fingal's Cave
16 Paul Gaughin (1848–1903)
17 Jamaica – he is Sir Noel Coward (1899–1973)
18 Devil's Island
19 Robinson Crusoe – created by Daniel Defoe
20 The flag of Chile
21 The Islands of Hawaii
22 The actress Lily Langtry – who was born in Jersey, one of the British Channel Islands
23 Faeroe Islands
24 The Duke of Windsor (1894–1972) – formerly Edward VIII, who was posted to the Bahamas after abdicating and marrying Mrs Simpson
25 Cyprus

74 · E · Pop Music

1 The Drifters
2 The Wailers – he is Bob Marley (1945–81)
3 Culture Club – he is lead singer Boy George
4 Paul McCartney
5 Ringo Starr
6 Jim Morrison (1943–71)
7 Cass Elliot (1943–77)
8 *Barbarella* – which featured a villain called Duran Duran, after whom the group named themselves
9 Nico
10 Bob Dylan
11 Dire Straits – he is Mark Knopfler
12 A billion – Alice Cooper's 1973 album was titled *Billion Dollar Babies*
13 Phil Spector
14 Peter Tork
15 *Play Misty for Me*
16 The Beach Boys
17 A Granny Smith
18 Waterloo – *Waterloo* was the title of Abba's Eurovision Song Contest hit, which links it with Waterloo Station and the site of the Battle of Waterloo
19 John Denver
20 Stewart Copeland
21 *Thriller* – by Michael Jackson, which had sold 35 million copies by May 1985
22 Chubby Checker – in 1960 (America) and 1962 (UK)
23 Warren Beatty
24 Motown
25 *My Way*

75 · H · Anniversaries

1 6 January
2 St Nicholas's
3 The signing of the Constitution in 1787
4 A grouse
5 Juliet – in *Romeo and Juliet*
6 4 July – Independence Day
7 Charles II – his birthday and date he returned from exile to London
8 1 March
9 John Keats
10 Hallowe'en
11 Walpurgis Night
12 St Swithin
13 St Andrew's Day – 30 November
14 St Patrick's Day – 17 March
15 1 May
16 31 May 1669
17 July – she was married to Prince Charles on 29 July 1981
18 9 August 1945
19 Henry VIII – the year was 1536 and the three wives were, in chronological order, Catherine of Aragon (1485–1536), Anne Boleyn (1504–36) and Jane Seymour (1509–37)
20 Jimmy Carter – the date is 1 October
21 The storming of the Bastille (1789)
22 Haiti – declared independent on 1 January 1804
23 St Valentine's Day – 14 February
24 Johann Sebastian Bach (1685–1750)
25 100 – both events occurred on 12 April, in 1961 and 1861 respectively

76 · AL · Names and Titles

1 *Richard III*
2 *The Lady Vanishes*
3 George Sand (1804–76)
4 *Gone With the Wind* – by Margaret Mitchell (1900–49)
5 Dorian Gray – in *The Portrait of Dorian Gray*
6 John Lennon's (1940–80)
7 *Penthouse*
8 A steam launch
9 Miss Jean Brodie – in *The Prime of Miss Jean Brodie* by Muriel Spark
10 Cleopatra – in *Antony and Cleopatra*
11 Michelangelo
12 *Pride and Prejudice*
13 Ellery Queen – the pseudonym of authors Frederic Dannay and Manfred B. Lee
14 *Twelfth Night*
15 Aphra Behn (1640–89)
16 Samuel Pepys (1633–1703)
17 Plato
18 Tinkerbell – who appears in *Peter Pan* by J. M. Barrie (1860–1937)
19 *The Inn of the Sixth Happiness*
20 Svengali
21 The Brothers Grimm
22 George Orwell (1903–50)
23 Salvador Dali
24 Bonaparte
25 Groucho Marx's (1890–1977)

77 · SN · Domestic Science

1 Four
2 68°F
3 20
4 Inventing the flush toilet
5 Paper patterns for dresses
6 Carbon dioxide, CO_2
7 The left
8 Six
9 Napoleon's army
10 Three
11 Salad dressing
12 Japan
13 One calorie
14 A two-bulb electric fire from 1911–12
15 Brewing tea automatically
16 The brassiere
17 Lavatory paper
18 Thomas Alva Edison in 1877
19 Barthélemy Thimmonier (1793–1854) – who invented a sewing machine in 1829
20 Melville R. Bissell
21 *Macbeth*
22 The television – which he invented using a mechanical system in 1925–26
23 Bulb
24 The bull's head opener
25 Walter Hunt

78 · SL · Water Sports

1 New South Wales – on Blowering Dam Lake
2 *Courageous*
3 The English Channel
4 Go
5 Backstroke races
6 Nine – eight oarsmen and one cox
7 c) 20 knots
8 The butterfly – which was separated from the breaststroke
9 Canada
10 Seven
11 The backstroke – he is John F. Kennedy
12 A ketch
13 Water skis
14 Self-contained underwater breathing apparatus
15 Olympic size
16 Ireland
17 Edward Heath – the yacht is *Morning Cloud*
18 The water ski
19 Perth
20 Synchronized swimming
21 A swimming pool
22 A white shark – weighing 2664 lb (1208.38 kg)
23 Clarence 'Buster' Crabbe
24 River Severn in England
25 Rowing – the star is Grace Kelly, who became Princess Grace of Monaco

79 · G · Down Under

1 The Southern Cross
2 Abel Tasman (1603–c.1659)
3 The Ross Dependency
4 Tasmania
5 The Great Barrier Reef
6 *The Sundowners* (1960)
7 Perth
8 Woomera
9 b) 1851
10 Ned Kelly (1855–80) – the picture shows Mick Jagger on television
11 A didgeridoo – it is an Aborigine instrument
12 Wellington is on the North Island
13 Barrie Humphries
14 Darwin
15 Walter Burley Griffin
16 The Nullarbor Plain in the south of Australia
17 Harold Holt
18 The Sydney Harbour Bridge
19 The Eureka Stockade
20 The North Island
21 The emu
22 The kiwi fruit
23 Olivia Newton-John
24 Ayer's Rock
25 Melbourne

80 · E · Stage Hits

1 *1776*
2 *Camelot*
3 *Porgy and Bess*
4 *Kismet*
5 *The Rocky Horror Show*
6 The Royal Shakespeare Company – the show is *Nicholas Nickleby*
7 Diane Keaton
8 *The Little Foxes*, by Lillian Hellman
9 *Grease*
10 *Barnum* – starring Michael Crawford
11 *The Elephant Man*
12 *Hair*
13 He appears as a hologram – the actor is Lord Olivier
14 Joel Grey
15 *Green Grow the Lilacs*
16 *Evita*
17 *Camelot*
18 Mark Twain (1835–1910)
19 *Bye Bye Birdie* – which was centred on Elvis Presley (1935–77)
20 *My Fair Lady*
21 *Becket*
22 Stephen Sondheim
23 George Gershwin (1898–1937) – with *Of Thee I Sing*
24 *Chess* – they are Tim Rice, Benny Andersson and Bjorn Ulvaeus
25 *Godspell*

81 · H · The Common People

1 Slavery
2 Franklin D. Roosevelt (1882–1945)
3 The House of Commons
4 The middle class
5 New York City
6 The Black Death, or Bubonic Plague
7 African slaves
8 Sharpeville
9 Cambodia – now Kampuchea
10 UNICEF
11 William Booth (1829–1912) – who founded the Salvation Army
12 Aaron Copland
13 *A Man For All Seasons*
14 Friedrich Engels (1820–95)
15 New Zealand – in 1893
16 Giuseppe Garibaldi (1807–82)
17 Marks and Spencer
18 *Liberté, Egalité, Fraternité*
19 Montgomery
20 Little Rock High School – Arkansas
21 Richard II (1367–1400) – the Peasants' Revolt took place in 1381
22 The Franco-Prussian War (1870–71)
23 The Commonwealth
24 The Atlantic Charter
25 He couldn't afford the fare – he is Karl Marx (1818–83)

82 · AL · Three Dimensions

1 Auguste Rodin (1840–1917)
2 Florence – in the Accademia
3 Furniture – he wrote *The Cabinet Maker's and Upholsterer's Drawing Book*
4 Peter Pan
5 Her arms
6 Mahogany
7 His *Pietà* – which was damaged in an attack
8 Gustave Eiffel (1832–1923) – the Eiffel Tower
9 Henry Moore – English sculptor
10 Le Corbusier (1887–1965)
11 The entrances to some metro stations
12 Sir Christopher Wren (1632–1723)
13 Benvenuto Cellini (1500–71)
14 Landscapes and gardens – his real name was Lancelot Brown (1716–83)
15 Sir Terence Conran
16 The Statue of Liberty – presented to America by the French in 1884
17 Sir Alec Issigonis – the car is the Mini, introduced in 1959
18 Brighton – it is the Brighton Pavilion, built in 1817 for the Prince Regent (later George IV)
19 Donatello (c.1386–1466)
20 Inigo Jones (1573–1652)
21 Bicycle handlebars
22 Sir Edwin Landseer (1802–73)
23 Charlton Heston
24 Wedgwood
25 The Bauhaus – a school of design founded by Walter Gropius in Germany, 1919

83 · SN · Motor Transport

1 The Stanley Steamer
2 The 'Tin Lizzie'
3 12 volts
4 Saturday
5 New York and Paris
6 Switzerland
7 The parking meter
8 Eddie Cochran
9 Henry Ford
10 *Goldfinger* – No. 24 is of course Sean Connery, alias James Bond
11 Lincoln Continental Executive
12 Mexico City
13 The Mini
14 Ferdinand Porsche (1875–1951)
15 A red flag
16 c) carburettor
17 Genevieve – which appeared in the movie of the same name
18 Lord Nuffield
19 Tread
20 Turin – FIAT stands for 'Fabbrica Italiana Automobili Torino'
21 Red – they changed to black during 1933
22 By an electric motor – the feat was achieved in 1899
23 Seat belts
24 Sir Clive Sinclair – inventor of the Sinclair C5
25 Isadora Duncan (1878–1927)

84 · SL · All American Sports

1 Horse racing
2 Judge Kenesaw Mountain Landis (1866–1944)
3 Eight seconds
4 Seven feet (2.13 m) tall
5 The Orange Bowl
6 Teddy Kennedy
7 Cricket and rounders – the game is baseball
8 The Boston Celtics
9 Tigers
10 The American League
11 Babe Ruth's
12 Arizona – the sport is rodeo
13 The centre
14 The Los Angeles Rams
15 Thurman Munson
16 The strike zone
17 Milwaukee's
18 Baseball
19 The Rose Bowl – played at Pasadena, California
20 Babe Ruth
21 Lacrosse
22 *The Winning Team*
23 The catcher's
24 A quarter of a mile (402.3 m) – they are drag racers
25 Canada's

85 · G · Farm Facts

1 Rhubarb and asparagus
2 Rice
3 The avocado
4 Truffles – a form of edible fungus
5 Wheat
6 The pea
7 Corn
8 Molasses
9 Cabbage
10 Beetroot
11 Green
12 Viticulture – the growing of grapes
13 The cabbage
14 Milk
15 Australia
16 Potatoes
17 Hops
18 Pink
19 He was a shepherd
20 The Archers
21 Tasmania
22 Eva Gabor
23 North Dakota
24 The USA – it's Clearwater Rice Inc., at Clearbrook, Minnesota
25 a) The sheep

86 · E · The Entertainers

1 Daniel Massey
2 Lenny Bruce's (1926–66)
3 Tom Jones
4 Schnozzle – he is Jimmy Durante (1893–1980)
5 Frank Sinatra
6 John Osborne
7 Sammy Davis Jr.
8 Coco the Clown
9 Will Rogers (1879–1935) – American comedian
10 Liverpool's Cavern Club – famous because The Beatles had played there in their early days
11 George Burns
12 Jim Henson – inventor of The Muppets
13 Kenny Everett
14 Fanny Brice (1891–1951)
15 The Marx Brothers
16 His violin
17 Bob Hope
18 Joan Rivers
19 Mae West (1893–1980)
20 Eddie Cantor (1892–1964)
21 The cowardly lion
22 1977 – he is Elvis Presley
23 George Jessel (1898–1981)
24 Victor Borge
25 Judy Carne

87 · H · Political Animals

1 John F. Kennedy (1917–63)
2 Sir Winston Churchill (1874–1965)
3 Jan Christian Smuts (1870–1950)
4 Manila, in the Philippines
5 James Monroe (1758–1831) – fifth American president. The capital is Monrovia
6 Adolf Hitler (1889–1945)
7 Theology
8 Abraham Lincoln (1809–65)
9 Napoleon Bonaparte (1769–1821) – the building is the Hôtel des Invalides
10 A Boeing 707
11 Niccolo Machiavelli's (1469–1527)
12 Henry Kissinger
13 Mexico
14 Simon Wiesenthal
15 Kenya
16 The *Queen Elizabeth II*
17 c) Ronald Reagan – who appears as a Nazi in *Desperate Journey*
18 The helicopter – he is Michael Heseltine, who resigned over the Westland affair
19 Nikita Khruschev (1894–1971)
20 Prince Otto von Bismarck (1815–98)
21 Gamel Abdel Nasser (1918–70)
22 He established the 49th parallel as the US-Canadian border
23 General Mohammad Zia ul-Haq
24 39
25 On his chin

88 · AL · Kids' Stuff

1 Tin Tin
2 Jack
3 100 years
4 A cat
5 Gotham City
6 Little Boy Blue
7 Marmalade sandwiches – he is Paddington Bear, created by Michael Bond
8 Giant Grumbo
9 A.A. Milne (1882–1956)
10 Ratty
11 University mathematics teacher – he is better known as Lewis Carroll (1832–98), author of *Alice in Wonderland*
12 A rose
13 West Germany
14 Darling
15 Willie Wonka – from *Charlie and the Chocolate Factory*
16 'A beautiful pea-green boat'
17 C.S. Lewis (1898–1963)
18 The Dormouse
19 Bashful
20 Bounce
21 Arthur Ransome (1884–1967)
22 P.L. Travers
23 *Cinderella*
24 Curds and whey
25 Shere Khan – the tiger

89 · SN · Ships

1 The *Queen Mary*
2 Three dots, three dashes, three dots in the Morse code devised by Samuel Morse (1791–1872)
3 Two fathoms, or 12 feet (3.6m) – it was the call of Mississippi pilots who sounded the river for shallow water
4 One
5 32
6 The *Calypso* – the scientist is Jacques Cousteau
7 The *Marie Celeste*
8 Green
9 The *Andrea Doria*
10 The *Bismarck*
11 The magnetic north
12 A son of a gun
13 The *Santa Maria*
14 The *Fram*
15 Humphrey Bogart (1899–1957) – the movie is *The Caine Mutiny* (1954)
16 a) 12lbs (5kg)
17 A rope supporting a mast or yard
18 She completed the first undersea round-the-world voyage
19 The *Turbinia*
20 RMS *Mauretania*
21 The intelligence ship *Pueblo* – captured by North Korea in 1968
22 Israeli – the destroyer *Eilat* was sunk by Egyptian fired missiles in October 1967
23 The Yangtze River
24 The *Mary Rose*
25 The Battle of Lepanto in 1571

90 · SL · Games

1 Whist
2 Blindman's buff
3 The Pluto Platter – better known as the Frisbee
4 25
5 50
6 The nine of hearts
7 28
8 Two
9 Five
10 Draughts, or checkers
11 25 points
12 Black and white
13 Rubik's Cube
14 A video game
15 Black
16 Tick-tack-toe
17 Three
18 Stones
19 The Philippines – it is the yoyo
20 The kaleidoscope
21 Sounds like
22 Mah-jong
23 Stage and Screen
24 *Risk's*
25 Right

91 · G · Organizations

1 Organization of African Unity
2 By banging his shoe on the table – he is Nikita Khrushchev (1894–1971)
3 Norwegian – Trygve Lie (1896–1968)
4 Organization of American States
5 c) 1949
6 Red Crescent
7 Paris
8 Donald Duck
9 T.H.R.U.S.H. – the picture shows David McCallum in *The Man From U.N.C.L.E.*
10 Australia, New Zealand and the USA
11 The Hague – Netherlands
12 Mexico – he is Fidel Castro
13 U Thant (1909–74)
14 France
15 Ecuador and Venezuela
16 The Netherlands's
17 Pope John XXIII
18 Rome – FAO stands for Food and Agricultural Organization
19 Vatican City (Holy See)
20 The Duke of Edinburgh
21 World Council of Churches
22 Philadelphia
23 The United Kingdom
24 Peace
25 Robert Baden-Powell (1857–1941) – the organization is the Boy Scouts

92 · E · Television

1 David Carradine
2 Kristin Shepard – the picture shows J.R., played by Larry Hagman in *Dallas*
3 Quentin Crisp's – the actor was John Hurt
4 St Elsewhere – from the TV show *St Elsewhere*
5 Michael Praed – who left *Robin of Sherwood* to join *Dynasty*
6 *Monty Python's Flying Circus*
7 Jack Lord
8 *Dempsey and Makepeace* – they are Glynis Barber and Michael Brandon
9 *Till Death Us Do Part*
10 K9
11 Hot Lips – the character is better known as Margaret Houlihan, played by Loretta Swit
12 Henry Winkler – shown as The Fonz in *Happy Days*
13 *The Phil Silvers Show*
14 *Bewitched*
15 Terry McCann and Arthur Daley – played by Dennis Waterman and George Cole
16 Dodge City
17 Five years
18 Derek Jacobi
19 *The Hitch Hiker's Guide to the Galaxy*
20 Lurch
21 Theo – the picture shows Telly Savalas, star of *Kojak*
22 Kermit
23 Lynda Carter – star of *Wonderwoman*
24 Mia Farrow
25 Herbert Lom

93 · H · Third World

1 Yugoslavian – she is Mother Teresa
2 Henry Morton Stanley (1841–1904)
3 Idi Amin
4 c) 1949
5 China
6 Mick Jagger
7 Mali
8 Gamal Abdel Nasser (1918–70)
9 Cuba
10 Salvador Allende (1908–73)
11 Jawaharlal Nehru (1889–1964)
12 The Zulus
13 A football match
14 Bangladesh
15 Saudi Arabia
16 Cambodia, or Kampuchea
17 The Dalai Lama's
18 Haiti – he is Baby Doc, alias Jean-Claude Duvalier, former president-for-life
19 Harold Macmillan
20 Paraguay
21 *The Dogs of War*
22 Tonga – he is King Taufa'ahau
23 Mozambique
24 La Réunion
25 Senegal

94 · AL · American Art and Architecture

1 Maine
2 Frank Lloyd Wright (1869–1959)
3 The Eskimos
4 a) The Hudson – Hudson River School
5 Mobiles
6 Samuel F.B. Morse (1791–1872)
7 Thomas Eakins (1844–1916)
8 Paul Revere (1735–1818)
9 Charles D. Gibson (1867–1944) – creator of the Gibson Girl
10 John Singer Sargent (1856–1925)
11 James McNeill Whistler (1834–1903)
12 Louis Comfort Tiffany (1848–1933)
13 Jackson Pollock (1912–56)
14 R. Buckminster-Fuller
15 Mount Rushmore National Memorial
16 Iowa
17 The Incas
18 Andy Warhol
19 American Primitive
20 Frederic Remington (1861–1909)
21 Anna Mary
22 Handball – in *Handball*
23 Man Ray (1890–1976) – a 'rayograph' is a picture made by placing an object against light sensitive paper
24 Mary Cassat (1844–1926)
25 Judy Chicago – whose work *The Dinner Party* celebrates women's struggles and achievements

95 · SN · Water Life

1 Ten
2 Tarka
3 Ivory
4 The shark's
5 A dolphin
6 Herring
7 The *Nautilus* – from *20 000 Leagues Under The Sea* by Jules Verne
8 Amity – the film is *Jaws*
9 The turtle – the album is *The Dream of the Blue Turtles*, and the artist is Sting
10 Mussels stewed with butter, white wine and shallots
11 A salmon
12 The crocodile
13 c) cartilage
14 A lobster
15 A jelly-fish
16 Three
17 Hergé
18 Plankton
19 The Russian sturgeon – valued for its caviare (roe)
20 The sardine
21 A calf
22 The ghavial or gavial – found in the rivers of India and Burma
23 Iceland
24 The coelacanth
25 By shooting a jet of water from the surface and knocking insects into the water

96 · SL · The Olympics

1 The women's marathon
2 Jock straps
3 Four – Winter and Summer Games in 1940 and 1944
4 Nikon
5 Baron Pierre de Coubertin (1863–1939)
6 Five continents
7 Longer – the marathon is 26 miles 385 yds (42.195 km)
8 Japan
9 West Berlin
10 South Africa
11 Paavo Nurmi (1897–1973)
12 Never
13 Coca Cola
14 One
15 Super heavyweight
16 France – in 1924
17 Sonja Henie (1910–69)
18 One
19 1984
20 Helsinki
21 Mick Jagger
22 Maple trees
23 Boxing – he is Errol Flynn
24 Princess Anne
25 Misha the bear

97 · G · Money Matters

1 Zurich
2 Life insurance
3 The dinar
4 Greece
5 The Louisiana Purchase from France in 1803
6 Japan's
7 Brazil
8 Guatemala's quetzal
9 From Spain – where the coins were stamped with an 8 to indicate the value of 8 reals
10 Zero
11 Japan
12 *Money, Money, Money* – by Abba
13 United Arab Emirates
14 Kentucky
15 Argentina
16 China, in AD 910
17 Jean Paul Getty (1892–1976)
18 Venezuela
19 Hungary
20 The estate of Howard Hughes (1906–76)
21 The Incas – who filled a hall for Francisco Pizarro with gold and silver in return for Atahualpa
22 *Cabaret* – she is Liza Minelli
23 Western Deep Level, Carletonville, South Africa
24 Ghana
25 Love – in the song *Can't Buy Me Love*

98 · E · Plays and Players

1 *The Mousetrap*
2 Sam Shephard
3 Morphine
4 Arthur Miller
5 Harold Pinter's
6 Oscar Wilde (1854–1900)
7 *Who's Afraid of Virginia Woolf*
8 *A Streetcar Named Desire* by Tennessee Williams – the actress was Vivien Leigh (1913–67)
9 *Equus*
10 Pope John Paul II
11 Samuel Beckett – the actress is Billie Whitelaw
12 Brendan Behan (1923–64)
13 *Statements After an Arrest Under the Immorality Act*
14 Godot – in *Waiting for Godot* by Samuel Beckett
15 *The Rivals* – by Richard Brinsley Sheridan (1751–1816)
16 *A Midsummer Night's Dream* – by William Shakespeare
17 Clifford Odets (1906–63)
18 Noh Theatre
19 Alan Ayckbourn
20 Neil Simon
21 The Method school
22 Bobby Watson
23 Antonio Salieri (1750–1825)
24 Noël Coward (1899–1973)
25 Hamlet – the actor is Sir John Gielgud

99 · H · Words and Ideas

1 Islam
2 Martin Luther King Jr. (1929–68)
3 In Mecca
4 Existentialism – the couple are Jean-Paul Sartre (1905–80) and Simone de Beauvoir (1908–85)
5 Seven
6 The Netherlands
7 Harry S. Truman (1884–1972)
8 Karl Marx (1818–83)
9 Mao Tse-tung (1893–1976)
10 Mormonism
11 Eat meat on a Friday
12 Adam Smith (1723–90)
13 Ludwig Wittgenstein (1889–1951)
14 Héloïse
15 'That's one small step for (a) man, one giant leap for mankind – first reported without the word 'a'
16 a) Confucius (551–479 BC)
17 The fear of the Lord
18 Roman Catholicism
19 The River Ganges
20 Réné Descartes (1596–1650)
21 Russia
22 John Paul I (1912–78)
23 Diogenes of Sinope (c.412–c.325 BC)
24 Thomas More (1478–1535)
25 Germaine Greer

100 · AL · The Classics

1 Sancho Panza
2 Cyrano de Bergerac
3 Esmerelda – in *The Hunchback of Notre Dame* by Victor Hugo (1802–85)
4 Emma
5 The Roman Empire – in *The Decline and Fall of the Roman Empire*
6 *Good Wives*
7 'Yo ho ho and a bottle of rum'
8 *Wuthering Heights*
9 In prison, in Bedford
10 Count Alexis Vronsky
11 Tobias Smollett (1721–71)
12 Donwell Abbey
13 *Far From The Madding Crowd*
14 Sir Walter Scott (1771–1832)
15 Alice Liddell (1852–1934) – in *Alice's Adventures in Wonderland* and *Through the Looking Glass* by Lewis Carroll
16 Mary Shelley (1797–1851) – in *Frankenstein*
17 Mrs Gaskell (1810–65)
18 *The Red Badge of Courage*
19 *Germinal*
20 *The White Peacock*, published in 1911
21 *Candide*
22 The Concord and Merrimac Rivers
23 Ivan Turgenev (1818–83)
24 Six
25 *Ulysses*

101 · SN · Astronomy

1 Jupiter's
2 Halley's comet
3 Aquarius
4 The Milky Way
5 Nicolas Copernicus (1473–1543)
6 Mercury
7 The moon
8 7 minutes 40 seconds
9 The corona
10 Venus
11 Tycho Brahe (1546–1601)
12 The Bonzo Dog Dooh-Da Band
13 The sun
14 a) Pluto
15 The Egyptians – he is Ra
16 One sixth
17 Three
18 David Bowie
19 Saturn
20 Sirius
21 Mars
22 The sun
23 Galileo Galilei (1564–1642) – he was forced to renounce his belief that the Earth revolved around the Sun by the Inquisition
24 Venus
25 Saturn

102 · SL · Food, Glorious Food

1 Water
2 Breadfruit trees
3 Sesame seed
4 The ewe (sheep)
5 Vichyssoise
6 Twice – 'biscuit' comes from the French *bis cuit* meaning twice cooked
7 Marco Polo – he brought pasta from China in the Middle Ages
8 Oliver – in *Oliver Twist*
9 c) 32 times
10 Honey
11 Clarence Birdseye (1886–1956)
12 a) Roast beef with 70 calories per ounce – roast veal has 65 and roast chicken 55
13 On the plains of North America – it is Jerusalem artichoke. It s partner is a globe artichoke
14 A tablespoon
15 Dried and salted fish – usually the bummalo
16 The herring family
17 Saffron
18 Bread sticks
19 A bouquet garni
20 Stuffed
21 Charles de Gaulle (1890–1970)
22 The pig – it is raw smoked ham served finely sliced
23 Julia Child
24 Music
25 Corn Flakes

103 · G · Where in the World

1 In Italy
2 Cape Cod
3 The Canary Islands
4 China
5 The Brandenburg Gate
6 The equator
7 Spain – in Granada
8 Utah
9 The Kimono
10 The Panama Canal
11 Belgium
12 Venice – it is the winged lion
13 Lebanon
14 The Nile
15 A cockney
16 Hong Kong
17 In Paris – in the film *Last Tango in Paris*
18 Stockholm
19 The Tower of London – they are Yeomen Warders
20 The Ukraine
21 In Philadelphia
22 Shah Jehan (1592–1666) – it is the Taj Mahal, built as a tomb for his favourite wife
23 Nigeria's
24 Grenada
25 Ethiopia's – the picture shows Bob Geldof founder of Band Aid and Live Aid

104 · E · Cops and Robbers

1 Six
2 The Sex Pistols – Ronald Biggs is one of the Great Train Robbers
3 *In the Heat of the Night*
4 Five
5 A guillotine
6 The French Connection
7 Captain Frank Furillo
8 They are brothers – they are Telly and George Savalas
9 Broderick Crawford
10 *Serpico* – the story was based on the true story of Frank Serpico
11 A diamond
12 *The Streets of San Francisco*
13 *Naked City*
14 *Police Woman* – the actress is Angie Dickinson
15 Officer Krupke
16 Dick Turpin
17 The Keystone Kops
18 Glenn Ford
19 Roger Daltrey
20 Jules
21 Adam Ant – who had a hit with *Stand and Deliver* in May 1981
22 Starsky
23 Chicago's
24 Sherlock Holmes
25 *Little Caesar* – the actor is Edward G. Robinson (1893–1973)

105 · H · World War II

1 American GI's in Britain
2 Spitfires
3 The attack on Pearl Harbor
4 Italy
5 Gestapo
6 Adolf Hitler
7 Japan and the USA
8 Operation Barbarossa
9 Noël Coward – the picture shows Admiral Earl Louis Mountbatten of Burma (1900–74)
10 Chunking
11 The USSR
12 Italy
13 The Channel Islands
14 HRH Queen Elizabeth, the Queen Mother – after Buckingham Palace was bombed
15 1940–on 10 May
16 In Normandy
17 A siren suit
18 Benito Mussolini (1883–1945)
19 Joseph P. Kennedy (1888–1969)
20 Vidkun Quisling (1887–1945)
21 Rudolf Hess
22 Egypt
23 The Utility Mark – which was stamped on goods from 1942 to signify a certain standard of design and quality
24 Operation Overlord
25 New Guinea

106 · AL · Shakespeare

1 Verona
2 Cole Porter (1893–1964) – the show was *Kiss Me Kate*
3 *Hamlet* – she is Agatha Christie (1891–1976)
4 Shylock
5 St George – the day is 23 April
6 A type of wine – generally white wines imported from Spain and the Canaries. Some were like sherry
7 He is killed by a bear
8 Sebastian
9 Akira Kurosawa
10 Miranda – in *The Tempest*
11 David Garrick (1717–79)
12 Puck
13 Henry Wrothesley, 3rd Earl of Southampton (1573–1624) – his patron
14 Duncan – King of Scotland
15 The Trojan War
16 Julius Caesar
17 HRH Prince Charles – who played Macbeth as a boy at Gordonstoun School
18 Richard Duke of Gloucester – later Richard III
19 *Henry V*, Act III scene 4
20 Hamnet
21 'my second best bed . . .'
22 *Romeo and Juliet* – the film is *West Side Story*
23 Beatrice
24 Egypt
25 The Forest of Arden

107 · SN · Railways

1 Works of art plundered by the Nazis
2 Mount Fuji in Japan
3 Casey Jones
4 Switzerland
5 France – TGV stands for Train de Grande Vitesse
6 In Australia – it runs for 297 miles (478 kms) across the Nullabor Plain
7 In Utah, at Promontory
8 The B.A.R.T. – Bay Area Rapid Transit System
9 He received the first actual golden disc on that date – he is Glen Miller (1904–44)
10 Mark Twain – the story was *Punch, Brothers, Punch*
11 J.M.W. Turner (1775–1851)
12 London, England
13 Colonel Nicholson – played by Alec Guinness
14 Moscow
15 Andrew Lloyd Webber – the musical is *Starlight Express*
16 At the rear – where it is a conductor's van
17 His was the first recorded fatality after a railway accident in 1830
18 The River Tay
19 Grand Central Station, New York City
20 Baltimore and Ohio
21 Rome's
22 A form of rail fastening
23 *Brief Encounter* – starring Celia Johnson and Trevor Howard, made in 1945
24 It's the longest in the world
25 Mr Norris – the novel is entitled *Mr Norris Changes Trains*

108 · SL · Sporting Greats – The Women

1 Vera Caslavska
2 Martina Navratilova
3 In Brazil
4 Hazel Wightman (née Hotchkiss) (1886–1974)
5 HRH Princess Anne
6 Water skiing
7 400 metres
8 Nadia Comaneci of Rumania – in 1976
9 Dawn Fraser of Australia
10 Lucinda Green (née Prior-Palmer)
11 Ice pairs
12 Billy Jean King
13 Esther Williams
14 The mile – she is Mary Decker-Slaney
15 Olga Korbut
16 c) 1900 – but only in the tennis and golf competitions
17 Sue Barker, of Britain
18 Dressage (riding)
19 Kathy Whitworth
20 Fanny Blankers-Koen of the Netherlands
21 In 1920
22 Ann Haydan Jones
23 Darts
24 Sonja Henie
25 She became the first woman ever to swim the English Channel

109 · G · Landmarks

1 Easter Island – the origin of the statues remains a mystery
2 The Ginza
3 France and Italy
4 Table Mountain
5 In Amsterdam – the Netherlands
6 In Singapore
7 Turkey – just inland from the Aegean, where it was a port in ancient times
8 Buckingham Palace
9 In Liverpool
10 On the coast of County Antrim, Northern Ireland
11 The Rockies
12 Lisbon – capital of Portugal
13 The Trevi fountain – in Rome
14 In Agra
15 The Champs Elysées
16 1600 Pennsylvania Avenue – it is the White House, home of the American president
17 The Suez (= Zeus) Canal
18 Martha's Vineyard, off the coast of Massachusetts
19 The Empire State Building
20 Red
21 The civilization of the Incas
22 The clock in St Stephen's Tower in the Houses of Parliament – often called Big Ben after the bell of the original name
23 Mississippi River – the Huey P. Long Bridge, at Melairie, Louisiana is 4.35 miles (7 km) long
24 The Spanish Steps
25 Hollywoodland – the site was originally intended for a real-estate development

110 · E · Comic Cuts

1 Snoopy
2 Asterix
3 *A Charlie Brown Christmas*
4 Robin – Batman's assistant
5 Spiderman
6 Krypton – he is Superman
7 Pogo
8 She's his first cousin
9 Huey, Dewey, Louie
10 Wimpy
11 *Yellow Submarine*
12 Sniff
13 Dino
14 Hagar
15 Snowy – the character is Tintin
16 Fritz the Cat
17 Roadrunner
18 Wonder Woman's
19 His spectacles
20 Donald Duck
21 His fiftieth birthday
22 The Penguin
23 Linus
24 Chic Young (1901–73)
25 Captain Marvel

111 · H · Origins

1 The brontosaurus
2 The blue whale
3 Charles Darwin (1809–82)
4 The horse
5 By land bridge from Siberia
6 In Germany – near Dusseldorf, in 1856
7 Palaeontology is the study of extinct animals and plants from fossil remains
8 The brick
9 The Triassic period
10 *One Million Years BC* – she is Raquel Welch
11 The okapi
12 Africa
13 Its 14 000 year old cave paintings
14 In Kenya
15 A mammoth
16 The Iron Age
17 The skull of Piltdown Man
18 Peking man – the Latin means 'the Chinese man of Peking'
19 Barney Rubble
20 Tyrannosaurus Rex – he is Marc Bolan, who died in 1977
21 *The French Lieutenant's Woman* – from the book by John Fowles
22 The supercontinent formed by all the world's landmass before it divided
23 The bat
24 Walt Disney
25 In New Zealand

112 · AL · Origins of English

1 Curfew
2 X
3 Unto – the abbreviation originally referred to the phrase 'I owe unto . . .'
4 Mongoose – more than one are mongooses
5 Son of
6 Books
7 The comma
8 Of
9 E
10 Thomas Bowdler (1754–1825) – he gave the world the word 'bowdlerize', which means to cut or edit a work prudishly
11 Dreamt
12 Z
13 Cleave
14 Rhythms
15 Opera
16 Jehovah
17 Gas
18 O.K.
19 Plural
20 Richard Nixon's
21 Absent Without Leave
22 Onomatopoeia – for example, the word *cuckoo* sounds like the bird it refers to
23 *The Rivals* (1775) – in which Mrs Malaprop appears, played here by Geraldine McEwen
24 Zenith
25 A spoonerism – named after Rev. William Archibald Spooner (1844–1930), dean and later warden of New College, Oxford

113 · SN · Signs and Symbols

1 Because
2 Bass clef
3 Carbon monoxide
4 Aries
5 The French Resistance – it is the Cross of Lorraine
6 Saturn
7 The ratio of the circumference to the diameter of a circle
8 Gold – *Aurum* in Latin
9 The Earth
10 Not equal to
11 Taurus
12 Ne represents the gas neon which is used in neon tubes and bulbs
13 Female
14 Pierre and Marie Curie – joint winners of the Nobel prize for Chemistry in 1903. The element is Radium
15 Infinity
16 Calcium
17 The moon's last quarter
18 Greater than
19 At; to
20 Male
21 The sun
22 Aquarius
23 Mg
24 Parallel
25 Libra

114 · SL · Ball Games

1 Earthball
2 Pele – real name Edson Arantes do Nascimento of Brazil
3 Pelota, or Jai Alai – the instrument is called a *chistera*
4 The yellow ball
5 The Ashes
6 Forest Hills
7 Four – the game is polo
8 Table tennis's
9 India
10 A softball
11 The Aztecs
12 The golf ball
13 Paddle rackets
14 The right
15 Softball
16 Red
17 Squash
18 Soccer's
19 Three times
20 Break service
21 a) Black
22 Badminton – it is played with a shuttlecock
23 Cliff Thorburn – Canadian snooker player
24 Rugby League has 13 players to Rugby Union's 15
25 Ireland's – the game is hurling

115 · G · Wastes and Wildernesses

1. Botswana
2. The Empty Quarter
3. Great Sandy Desert – with an area of 160 000 miles² (420 000 km²) to the Nubian Desert's 100 000 miles² (260 000 km²)
4. Greenland – it is Godthaab
5. c) 1911
6. Bactrian camel (with two humps)
7. The deserts of Australia, which they explored
8. The west
9. Theodore Roosevelt
10. India and Pakistan
11. A sheep – 'Ovis Poli', or Marco Polo sheep
12. The Andes at 4500 miles (7200 km)
13. Spanish – a member of the 1540 expedition led by Francisco Vazquez de Coronado
14. Chile and Argentina
15. *Nanook of the North*
16. The Tuareg
17. Almost six weeks. He spent forty days in the wilderness.
18. a) ½ – it is roughly half the size of Africa: 11 506 000 miles² (29 800 000 km²) to c.5 500 000 miles² (c.13 600 000 km²)
19. Gary Cooper
20. On Antarctica – the Lambert-Fisher Ice Passage is c.320 miles (515 km) long
21. Great Bear Lake at 12 275 miles² (31 800 km²) to Lake Ontario's 7520 miles² (19 500 km²)
22. The Sahara
23. *Zabriskie Point*
24. The Hejaz Railway
25. Alice Springs

116 · E · Words and Music

1. *Things We Said Today*
2. Oklahoma!
3. *Your Song*
4. Yellow polka dot bikini
5. *All I Really Want To Do*
6. The fruit of the poor lemon
7. *Aquarius*
8. *Cecilia*
9. That was the day Buddy Holly died
10. *She Loves You* and *All You Need Is Love*
11. *San Francisco*
12. An Island in the Sun – he is Harry Belafonte
13. Through the streets of London
14. Joe DiMaggio
15. Barbara Ann
16. Deborah Kerr – who played Anna
17. Sting – of Police
18. John F. Kennedy (1917–63) – the singer is Frank Sinatra
19. My blue suede shoes
20. 'Que sera sera', whatever will be will be' – from the song *Whatever Will Be Will Be*
21. Do wah diddy diddy dum diddy do
22. Lily the Pink – they are *Scaffold*
23. Hernando's
24. *Substitute*
25. Sonny Bono – the singer is Cher

117 · H · Heroes and Heroines

1. Lord Byron (1788–1824)
2. Fly solo across the Atlantic – she is Amelia Earhart (1898–1937) who flew from Newfoundland to Burry Point, Wales
3. Amelia Bloomer (1818–94) – who gave her name to an early type of women's trouser
4. Switzerland – William Tell is widely thought to have led a drive for Swiss independence in the Middle Ages
5. Bob Geldof's
6. Electrician – he is Lech Walesa, one of the founders of the Solidarity movement
7. *Much Ado About Nothing*
8. Hatshepsut – 18th Dynasty Egyptian ruler who defied tradition to lead her country
9. Boadicea or Boudicca – queen of the Iceni tribe in the 1st century AD, who led her army against the Romans
10. Martin Luther King Jnr (1929–68) – who was assassinated in Memphis, Tennessee, while on a civil rights mission
11. In China, where he quelled the Taiping rebellion
12. The Unknown Soldier – the picture shows the Arc de Triomphe in Paris
13. Moshe Dayan (1915–81)
14. Prince Charles Edward Stewart (1720–88) – also known as the Young Pretender and Bonny Prince Charlie. He escaped after the Battle of Culloden (1746) disguised as Flora Macdonald's maid
15. Marie Curie (1867–1934) – who discovered radium and died of leukemia after absorbing dangerous doses of it during her experiments
16. Edith Cavell (1865–1915)
17. Captain Lawrence Oates (1880–1912) – who, convinced that his frostbite would handicap the rest of the party in their bid to reach safety, sacrificed his life
18. Malta's – because of their fortitude in the face of heavy bombing
19. The French Resistance
20. Horatio Nelson (1758–1805)
21. Joan of Arc (1412–31)
22. Paul Revere (1735–1818) – hero of the American Revolution
23. Portugal's
24. Pocahontas (1595–1617) – who twice saved the life of Captain John Smith
25. Grace Darling (1815–42) – daughter of William Darling, a lighthouse keeper

118 · AL · Women in Print

1. Pills
2. *Peyton Place*
3. *Gone With The Wind*
4. Yoko Ono
5. Pink – she is Barbara Cartland, romantic novelist
6. *Lace* – the author was Shirley Conran, author of the *Superwoman* books
7. New Zealander
8. Agatha Christie (1891–1976)
9. Alice Walker – the book and film are *The Color Purple*
10. Billie Holliday's
11. *A House is Not a Home*
12. Germaine Greer
13. Maya Angelou's
14. Stevie Smith (1902–71)
15. Agatha Christie (1891–1976)
16. Anne Frank's
17. Edna O'Brien's
18. Shirley MacLaine
19. Mrs Isabella Beeton (1836–65)
20. Elinor Glynn (1864–1943)
21. Daisy Ashford
22. Kathleen Mansfield (1888–1923)
23. Doris Lessing
24. Karen Blixen – the film is *Out of Africa*
25. Ann Jellicoe

119 · SN · Eureka

1. The electric battery – the volt is named after the Count (1745–1827)
2. Zip fastener
3. German – Johann Gutenberg (c. 1400–68) invented it c. 1455. His 42 line Latin Bible is illustrated
4. Locksmith
5. Louis Pasteur (1822–95)
6. St John's – Newfoundland
7. George Stephenson (1781–1848) – inventor of the *Rocket* railway locomotive
8. The monkey wrench
9. The electric razor – first manufactured 18 March 1931
10. Thomas Alva Edison (1847–1931)
11. c) 1953 – by the Dunlop Rubber Company
12. Benjamin Franklin (1706–90)
13. Microscope – a compound convex-concave lens
14. Condensed milk
15. His wife's hand
16. George Mortimer Pullman (1831–97)
17. Machine gun – called the Gatling gun
18. Alexander Graham Bell (1847–1922)
19. Margarine – named after *margarites* by Hippolyte Mège-Mouriez, patented 1869
20. Taking a bath
21. The computer
22. Frozen food
23. Nylon
24. Roulette wheel
25. Charles Macintosh (1766–1843)

120 · SL · Winter Sports

1. Bill Johnson – in 1984 with a new Olympic speed record
2. Skiing
3. St Moritz
4. Swedish
5. Anchorage – Alaska
6. *Help!*
7. It's been touched
8. A ski-bob
9. Women's giant slalom
10. British – he was Squadron Leader Mike Freeman, bobsleigher and flag bearer at the 1972 Winter Olympics
11. Toes
12. Kitzbühel
13. Lake Placid
14. Mount Everest
15. Sierra Nevada
16. Princess Andrew, Duchess of York
17. Grenoble
18. Sapporo – Japan
19. Because it's called the Inferno, the name Dante gave to part of his *Divine Comedy*
20. Maurice Ravel (1875–1937) – they are Jayne Torvill and Christopher Dean
21. b) 610 ft (186 m)
22. The highest on skis – 129.30 mph (208.09 km/h), as opposed to 80 mph (128 km/h) on a toboggan
23. Norwegian
24. Fridtjof Nansen (1861–1930) – Norwegian explorer
25. *The Spy Who Loved Me*